Praise for the Auth…

'I still remember when in colleges Indian cuisine was synonymous with Chef Satish Arora. He is a true custodian of our culinary heritage. Thank you, Chef, for being our guide for fifty glorious years at the Taj.'

—Vikas Khanna

'Chef Satish Arora is a most humble chef with a stellar professional career. If ever there was a chef I would love to be other than who I am then it has to be him. I am honoured to know him closely and blessed to have learned a lot from him. Through this book, much like in his life, he charms, engages and entertains.'

—Sanjeev Kapoor

'I have known Chef Arora even before joining the hotel industry and he has been my role model for the twenty-eight-plus years that I have been with hotels. His biography is a beautiful and interesting insight into the life of a legend.'

—Ranveer Brar

'Chef Satish Arora is truly a culinary icon of India. When I joined the Taj Group in 1996, he was the one we looked up to. I have learned so much from his legacy. He is one of the founding fathers of modern chefs; he led the way for so many of us. He has had a major impact on young chefs for many decades now. I congratulate him on his book.'

—Manish Mehrotra

'Chef Satish, you always inspire your colleagues and young culinarians to showcase their ability and work, and with this book I am sure you will set another milestone for the future. As the president of the World Association of Chefs' Societies, with millions of chefs around the globe, I want to congratulate you on your hard work, dedication and endless passion for food.'

—Thomas A. Gugler, president of the
World Association of Chefs' Societies

'Chef Satish Arora is a true icon of Indian cuisine. He is a once-in-a-generation talent, whose loyalty is absolutely unparalleled. Having spent more than fifty-five years at the famed Taj Group, where he became the world's youngest executive chef to handle a five-star hotel kitchen at the age of twenty-six, Satish Arora has since trained over 5,000 young chefs who've gone on to work in prestigious restaurants around the world. *Sweets and Bitters* is a gripping, truly mesmerising read: the fascinating story of a chef whose influence continues to change the way a whole generation of chefs approach Indian cuisine.'

—Atul Kochhar

'Chef Satish Arora has been the guiding light for many chefs of my generation. A legendary chef who has cooked for many dignitaries, royalty included, but also someone who showed us how regional Indian food, scrumptious home-style cooking, can be recreated to suit restaurant menus. His undying passion for Indian food is something that has left a deep impression on my mind.'

—Vineet Bhatia

SWEETS AND BITTERS

SWEETS AND BITTERS

Tales from a Chef's Life

Satish Arora
as told to Chandrima Pal

Foreword by Vir Sanghvi

BLOOMSBURY
NEW DELHI • LONDON • OXFORD • NEW YORK • SYDNEY

BLOOMSBURY INDIA
Bloomsbury Publishing India Pvt. Ltd
Second Floor, LSC Building No. 4, DDA Complex, Pocket C – 6 & 7,
Vasant Kunj, New Delhi 110070

BLOOMSBURY, BLOOMSBURY INDIA and the Diana logo
are trademarks of Bloomsbury Publishing Plc

First published in India 2023
This edition published 2023

ISBN: PB: 978-93-88630-80-1; e-ISBN: 978-93-88630-82-5
2 4 6 8 10 9 7 5 3 1

Typeset in Fournier MT Std by Manipal Technologies Limited
Printed and bound in India by Thomson Press India Ltd

MIX
Paper from responsible sources
FSC® C010615

To find out more about our authors and books, visit www.bloomsbury.com and sign up for our newsletters

To Sushma, my wife, the rock of my life, generous to a fault. It is her quiet strength and unwavering support that have helped me live my dreams.

To the Taj Group of Hotels, for making a chef out of a food-loving Delhi boy.

CONTENTS

FOREWORD

I still remember when I first met Chef Satish Arora. I had just finished school, was waiting to go up to university and was killing time writing journalistic articles. Arora was much older and more experienced but he was, in some ways, a bit of a newcomer himself.

He had taken over as executive chef of The Taj Mahal Hotel a few years previously and was struggling to make his mark. For one, he was absurdly young. Having been appointed to the post when he was in his mid-twenties, he may well have been the youngest chef ever to run the kitchens of a luxury hotel with so many restaurants, anywhere in the world.

Arora was part of a new generation of chefs who had studied at catering college and wanted to impose the exacting standards of a great French kitchen on what had traditionally been an old-style operation where the chefs had joined the hotel as vegetable choppers and picked up cooking techniques along the way. Because Arora was so much younger than them, had come from a Delhi catering college and was a Punjabi, the Goans and Parsis who had dominated the Taj's restaurants and kitchens for decades were unwilling to take him seriously.

It did not help that he had succeeded the legendary Masci—Chef Miguel Mascarenhas—who, though he had stepped down after decades as the hotel's top chef, still came to the kitchen every day to a warm reception from the adoring team he had hired.

Arora does not talk about those days much, preferring to focus on his later triumphs but I reckon all Indian chefs owe him a huge debt of gratitude for the manner in which he professionalised the Taj's kitchens, imposing order where there had once been a free-for-all and making it clear that knowing how to cook was not enough. For a kitchen to consistently turn out good food, the brigade had to be disciplined.

There had been expatriate chefs at Indian hotels before. Delhi's Oberoi Intercontinental, India's first modern five-star hotel, predated the professionalisation of the Taj and the inauguration of its new wing by seven years but the Delhi hotel relied on the Intercontinental systems and foreign managers and chefs—one reason why few of its early chefs are remembered today.

But though the Taj had a marketing arrangement with Intercontinental for its tower wing, which opened in 1972, its management was solidly Indian. And Arora was the first Indian chef to be put in charge of such a massive restaurant complex.

It helped, I think, that Arora was not just a great chef, he was also a born cook. The older chefs in the Taj's kitchens were gobsmacked when he would demonstrate that he could cook virtually any dish better than they could. Grudgingly, they began to respect his skills and fell in line.

And it helped that he was flexible and adaptable. At catering college, he had been a favourite of Roger Moncourt, the legendary French chef who laid the foundations of European cuisine in India. By the time Arora joined the Taj he knew how to cook with cream and wine. But the challenges at the Taj were different. The hotel was so proud of being Indian that it wanted to serve the sort of Indian food that five-star hotels did not usually bother with.

We remember Arora for introducing the South Indian breakfast menu that is now a staple of Indian hotels. But we forget how much he experimented with lighter dishes that built on Indian flavours. At the Shamiana coffee shop, he introduced a series of Indian hamburgers with such names as spicy mutton burger. His most famous invention was the now ubiquitous chilli cheese toast, for which he rarely gets the credit he deserves. But he also invented the first chicken tikka sandwich, now a global standard, putting it on the menu as the room service special.

Over the years, as the Taj expanded to become India's leading hotel chain, Arora took his skills to other hotels. At the Fort Aguada in Goa, he was instrumental in creating a Goan menu that all Goan restaurants still serve. The Fort Aguada was Goa's first modern hotel. Till that point nobody had codified Goan dishes and worked out how to serve them in upmarket surroundings.

Nor were his skills restricted to India. When the Taj began looking at an expansion into Sri Lanka, Arora became fascinated by the food of that country. He was the first chef to serve egg hoppers in India, and the first to tell Indians what lampreys were.

I could go on. But I imagine this book will provide all the details and capture the depth of Arora's contribution to Indian food and to the hotel industry.

Till the end of his time at the Taj, he never tired. When he finally moved away from hotel kitchens, the Taj sent him to turn around its unprofitable flight catering unit. I was not surprised when he made it a profit centre. And as private airlines took off, Arora and the Taj set the standard for what such newcomers as Jet Airways served first-class passengers.

He turned up in the oddest places. I once bumped into him in the lobby of New York's Waldorf Astoria hotel. He was part of Prime Minister Atal Bihari Vajpayee's party and, along with other Taj chefs, was expected to turn out the best Indian food for the prime minister's guests. There was no tradition of cooking Indian food in the Waldorf Astoria's kitchens but Arora created an Indian corner. Each morning he would fry Indian spices so that their aromas filled his corner. That made him feel he was back home in India and not in some strange New York kitchen. And once he felt at home, great dishes kept coming.

My lasting memory of Arora is his love for cooking. If I ever called him and asked a simple question, for instance, 'Chef, what is a Hyderbadi biryani?' he would never offer me a single description. Instead, his reply would nearly always begin with 'First, you chop some onions, then you heat some fat . . .'

Chef Satish Arora loves to cook. And he taught India's chefs to cook. His contribution will never be forgotten.

Vir Sanghvi, author and food critic

PROLOGUE

Atal Bihari Vajpayee and Indira Gandhi, two of our legendary prime ministers, not only held very divergent political views but nurtured very different approaches towards food. If the former happily went with the flow, using his fingers to pop a crunchy pani puri into his mouth and even licking a tangy chutney off his fingers, the latter was all about method, presentation, detailing and perfection—fruits had to be just ripe, precisely cut in a certain way; meals once planned could not be changed. But both these remarkable individuals had something in common—they respected and appreciated every plate of food that was placed before them. I am perhaps one of the very few people alive who can tell you just how much spice was enough for one, or how the other liked her papaya for breakfast.

Or, for that matter, how despite her prim and proper image and gravitas, the Queen of England had a childlike curiosity about cooking techniques and loved her curries. Her husband, Prince Philip, had a discerning palate and could easily tell the flavours of one culinary region from the other, and even handle spicy, Indian food with ease! On the other hand, Mr J.R.D. Tata preferred subtle flavours, fresh herbs for his grilled fish and meat, which he savoured at lunch. Former President of the United States (POTUS) Bill Clinton, however, happily swapped his fancy cutlery for his fingers to get the most of the raan and brinjal dishes I prepared for him.

Through this book, I will take you inside the rough and tumble of the flight kitchens that worked round the clock to put hot, delicious meals on tray tables and tell you about planning the historic launch of Starbucks in India—where we came up with an Indian menu that had to match up to the brand's international standards and legacy. There are also the stories about my brief but eye-opening encounters with global celebrity chefs, Gordon Ramsay and Wolfgang Puck; setting up prestigious restaurants showcasing our glorious Indian food all over the world, and bringing home the top honours from the world—such as the Gold Medal at the Culinary Olympics held in Japan or being inducted into the Hall of Fame by the Indian Federation of Culinary Associations.

Even after all the decades I spent in the most famous kitchen of the world, mornings at my residence, a whisper away from The Taj Mahal Palace, Mumbai, begin with a glimpse of the splendorous dome of the magnificent building where it all began. The Taj Mahal Palace Hotel may be a historic, cultural and architectural marvel to most people, one of India's most loved and respected icons of hospitality, but for me, it is a place that has been my temple, where I spent the best and the most fulfilling decades of my life learning, growing, cooking and serving with pride and love.

Every time I walk into the Taj, I feel like I am coming home.

Whenever I step into the lobby, familiar faces greet me. In the restaurants, I know every nook and corner, every table and every countertop. Even if you blindfold me in the kitchens, I can tell you where to find the rice and the flour, the lentils or the lobsters. The soul of the Taj kitchen has remained the same even after its layout has been changed many times. The soul that revealed itself to me only after tossing me into the fire and grilling me to perfection.

I know these walls, I know the walk, I know I am home. My home of over fifty years. The place where I began my journey as a trainee and became the world's youngest executive chef at a five-star hotel. It is here that I cooked for the most famous, most celebrated and the most discerning guests. It is also here that I first discovered my passion for Indian cuisine, reimagined for a global palate—such as the Chicken Tikka Sandwich served at a five-star high tea service for the first time.

From being a nervous trainee to becoming one of the longest-serving executive chefs in the hospitality industry—travelling the world, cooking for prime ministers, presidents, film stars and alongside celebrity chefs—I feel humbled to have been on a culinary journey that is rich, diverse, full of flavour and all soul.

Spread over five decades, many continents and as many dishes, this is my story—one of a frail and mischievous boy from Delhi who didn't even know what a sprig of parsley looked like before he stepped into a commercial kitchen and acquired the confidence to cater to some of the most well-known people with the most refined tastes in the world.

I

Arbi Chaat, Palak Pakoda, Matka Kulfi

The taste of my childhood

My most vivid and precious memories of my mother, Pushpa Arora, are from the kitchen, where I used to watch her create magic out of the mundane. With her bright eyes, stocky frame that was always upright and her shoulders squared and ready to take on every curveball that life threw at her, she was the picture of someone who always held things together with a smile and a touch of tadka.

Born and raised in Rawalpindi (now in Pakistan's Punjab province), my mother was a simple and pious woman. The eldest of five sisters, she was extremely soft-spoken, docile and a good student at school. Perhaps if she had been encouraged to pursue her interests, she would have excelled in academics or any other vocation. But Mummy ji, as we called her, did exactly as was expected of any good Indian girl in those days—she followed time-honoured family traditions and got married early, to a man chosen by her parents, Om Prakash Arora. The Arora family later migrated to Jalandhar and finally settled in Delhi.

I was born in Delhi, and we lived in a modest, middle-class house—functional and hardly ostentatious. And the kitchen was a reflection of this life philosophy. Small but neatly planned, it was stacked with steel and glass dabbas full of aromatic spices, dals and dried herbs, stainless steel pots and pans that sparkled after being scrubbed clean; ladles, strainers, tawas and kadhais that would cater to the hunger pangs of a family with three growing children. But in the eyes of my six-year-old self, it was a magical place of endless wonders.

I can still visualise my mother in action in our family kitchen in in a nondescript middle-class neighbourhood near Paharganj, Delhi, where we grew up. On cold winter days, we would warm up at the aroma of paalak, methi and pyaaz. I can see Mummy ji with the straining ladle, gently tapping the fritters as they danced in a kadhai full of bubbling oil. On Sundays and holidays, she used to make pakodas for breakfast with fresh seasonal, flavourful vegetables. Paalak ka pakoda, aaloo ka pakoda, baingan, gobhi, mirchi, pyaaz—anything and everything could be coated in spicy batter and fried to a perfect, golden crispiness. I simply loved her pakodas and we made a small celebration of the meal by sitting in a circle in the large courtyard, on a chatai or chador as Mummy served the pakodas to us kids—hot off the kadhai. My happiest food memories go back to these days. My brother, who was not as passionate about food, would not show the same kind of enthusiasm as my sister and I did. In fact, not only did I polish off my share, I would dig into my sister's share as well—especially if there were paalak and gobhi ones, my favourites.

Mummy ji would chide me affectionately, calling me the naughty one who not only gobbled up his share, but was always eyeing that of his siblings!

She was my first guru. She not only fuelled my curiosity for food, but also nurtured the food lover in me. Whenever I had the opportunity, I would sit in the kitchen, watching

Mummy ji conjure up the most delicious dishes with the most imperceptible sleight of hand. Though we never quite acknowledged it, today I can say it with much pride that my mother's kitchen was actually the heart of our family, and our lives flowed to the gentle rhythm of her hands.

Other than the bhajias and pakodas, Mummy ji was also fond of making kulfis. The day she would come back from the bazaar with matkas, my heart would do a little jig at the sight of those small earthen pots—I knew we were in for a treat the next day. It was not merely my duty to wash the matkas, I would insist on doing so! Mummy taught me how important it was to soak the matkas overnight to avoid the muddy smell from creeping into the kulfi. That warning was enough to make me rinse and soak the matkas diligently as if my life depended on it.

Kulfi prepping usually happened between 2 and 5 PM—that golden hour between lunch and dinner. It worked for me—I was usually back from school by 1 PM and would wait eagerly for her to start boiling the milk. The aroma of pure cow's milk bubbling and frothing on the stove heralded the onset of the elaborate kulfi-making process.

I would watch my mother sit on her haunches, patiently stirring the milk, so that it wouldn't stick to the bottom of the pan. There was no concept of heavy-bottomed pans in those days, and getting the result you desired was all a matter of one's skill. How you moved the ladle, how often you stirred, how you controlled the heat, was all evident in the taste of the finished kulfi.

It was not until I was a teenager that I began to ask her questions about the process—why did she reduce the milk?

'It helps set the kulfi better,' she would reply.

'Why do you add kheer to it?' I was curious about the well-cooked kheer that she added to the condensed milk.

'If I don't, the kulfi will become icy in the centre.' She explained her little trick to ensure the kulfi remained soft and creamy.

Honestly, I did not care at the time if this was traditional wisdom or my mother's innovation. All I knew was this—the kheer in the kulfi tasted divine! And while for the rest of the family it was simply just another tasty dessert that my mother had perfected, for me, it was also a learning. And this learning, along with the joy that dry fruits-enriched, creamy kulfi brought to my little life, extended to everything that came out of my mother's kitchen. Chana, rajma, sarson ka saag, aloo ka paratha, makai ki roti…

I remember once when my mother fell sick and it was such a nightmare for me. All I could think of was—Kaun, kya, kaise? Who would do the cooking and how? There was no concept of part-time help or a cook-for-hire in those days.

On such occasions, it would be the grandmothers and single aunts who would come to the rescue of the family. So my Nani, who used to stay near our house, and my single aunt were called to help out with the cooking and feeding of the three children of the Arora household. I was terribly unhappy, even miserable—I found their cooking not a patch on that of my mother's. It was also frustrating to see that the other family members did not share my feelings. I registered my protest by sulking and generally being insufferable!

If you think that this devotion towards Mummy ji's cooking kept me away from experimenting with other culinary delights that awaited me out there in the big, wide world, you'd be mistaken. All through my school life, right up to my college days, I would never let go of an opportunity to indulge in street food. And Delhi is a Mecca of street food.

I was a fan of everything from deep-fried samosas and tangy chaats and pani puri, to the medley of pakodas sold by the thelawalas—fluffy, golden bhature with flavourful black chole, yellow dal that packed a solid punch with the red chillies and asafoetida, wholesome rajma chawal, soft kulcha and sour and spicy imli chole from Chandni Chowk; moong dal laddoos that crumbled between your fingers, besan ka chilla stuffed with paneer, tille-wali kulfi, keema kulcha prepped on tawas and swimming in oil, gurda kapura (offals cooked in a medley of spices), chicken boti (gizzards and intestines) masala. There was an astounding variety of lip-smacking junk food to choose from, all through the year. Especially during the long and severe winters in the city.

Even though I absolutely loved my mother's cooking, I would often convince her that my school routine that day did not allow me to take packed food from home. My mother was naive enough to believe me, which would allow me to sneakily spend my pocket money on the delicious, colourful, spicy, oily food from the carts and the hole-in-the-wall joints of yore. But when it came to catering to my love for chatpata food, my mother would trump the street food vendors in her own way.

Mummy ji, whose knowledge of food and cooking techniques was born and honed in the home kitchen, showed remarkable ingenuity when it came to giving familiar dishes a quirky twist. One such dish that caught my fancy, especially during my professional career, was the tali-hui arbi or fried colocasia. My mother was very fond of arbi. And while for most people it was an acquired taste, she found a way of making it exciting and palatable for us.

The small but delicious flourishes that I learned in my mother's kitchen have stayed with me all these years. I am yet to come across a chaat made with crisp-fried arbi, tomatoes and spicy jackfruit curry with jackfruit seeds in it. And it is for this alone that I consider her to be my culinary guru.

My parents were seldom part of our family food rituals. My father mostly kept to himself. He preferred to bury himself in his spiritual books and newspapers, only occasionally joining the rest of the family for meals or snacks. Mummy ji would hurriedly eat in the kitchen because our elaborate morning breakfasts left her with little time to prepare for lunch. The custom of the family dining at the table was quite a rare thing in those days. In fact, families bonded when they sat together, cross-legged on the floor, eating the food served hot by the matriarch of the family. We didn't even have a dining table, to begin with!

My father would come home in the evenings and have his dinner early, by 6:30 PM or so. But we kids used to eat later with Mummy. The mood was always warm and jovial. Hindi film songs playing on the radio, us sharing the food, cracking jokes, laughing. On Wednesdays, with my trusted transistor by our side, we would all listen to Amin Sayani's *Binaca Geet Mala*. All three of us were so crazy about it that every week, we used to predict the top songs for the week! Music, food and banter was the glue that held the Arora family kids and their mother together.

My mother had not had much social exposure, having led an orthodox, cloistered life, but what she did have was an eye for detail, a natural flair for mixing and matching ingredients, a deep reverence for seasonal produce and intuitive mastery over the fine art of cooking. She may not have cooked for famous people, but she cooked for the people she loved, with a lot of love. And when you cook with love, for love, it shows in every little thing that passes through your hands. Even a glass of lassi or a bowl of dal.

It is thanks to the hours spent observing my mother that I learnt how to pick the right kind of vegetables for a particular recipe, how each dish requires a different cut of the same vegetables, how Indian masala or spices react to heat and oil, and when and how to use Indian herbs to unlock their aroma and enhance their healing properties.

My mother and I loved to exchange ideas. Rather, I would cajole her into trying out different dishes with the same old ingredients, because I liked variety.

'Mummy ji, why do we use makai (Indian corn) always in the same way? Why not use it in a dessert?'

She would either laugh my suggestion off, or actually try and come up with something new—like bhutte ki kheer! She was an instinctive and creative cook who paid attention to every little element that comprised a dish. So much so that even a simple dish of mattar paneer would taste extraordinary. I looked forward to our meals and our conversations around them.

In my early teens—when my love for food and my curiosity about cooking techniques and recipes first began to take shape—I would come home from school early and if my mother was away at any of her religious gatherings, I would seize the opportunity to sneak into the kitchen. Left to my own devices, I would try and cook up a suji ka halwa or upma or kheer. I would then wait for my mother excitedly.

As soon as Mummy ji would step into the house, she would know something was cooking. Literally! She would sniff the air and say, 'What's that fragrance? Have you been cooking something again?'

'Haan ji, Mummy ji.' I would then proudly produce my handiwork.

My mother would feign anger, but you could hear affection dripping from every word she uttered. 'Why do you get into the kitchen? It's a woman's job,' she would reprimand me.

It is important to understand that we are talking about a different time here. A different world. And my mother was a product of a culture that looked down upon men who volunteered to do what were considered to be solely women's jobs. And this included all kitchen chores.

Sometimes, my mother would playfully scold me and sometimes, if I made a mistake, she would teach me, even as she continued scolding me. 'You have put too much water! You have ruined the dish! This is not how you do it!' she would say.

That is how I learned. From my mistakes. From my mother's affectionate reprimands. Even if she was uncomfortable with my forays into the kitchen, she never really stopped me from cooking. And so I continued with my experiments. I began to note down the different recipes I tried out.

I have always been a staunch believer in maintaining little diaries. Just as I wrote down everything about a meal here or a sweet treat there, I would also note down observations about my everyday life. If I saw something new on family holidays, the occasions when my brother did something mischievous or when my father lost his temper. It is a habit that has stayed with me till date.

I created a recipe book of sorts with my mother's cooking tips. When she used to scold me for a porridge that was too runny or a dish that was too salty, I would note my mistake down, so that I would not repeat it.

To be honest, I don't think my mother was eager to enlist my help in the kitchen. Even then, I used to offer to help with even the smallest of tasks, whether it was peeling the carrots, shelling the peas or chopping the onions.

'Mummy ji, I am done with my homework, can I help you?' I would ask. Then I would chat her up on the pretext of helping around. We shared a special bond in the kitchen. Maybe she appreciated it—my being around in the kitchen, talking to her. At least I would like to think as much.

2

High Third Class

My grandfather Mukund Lal was a station master in a city formerly called Montgomery (now Sahiwal) in the Punjab province of East Pakistan. My father, Om Prakash, was the eldest of five siblings; an intelligent young man and a good student who excelled in English and Mathematics. In Delhi, he joined the civilian branch of the Army Headquarters before moving to the Judge Advocate General (JAG) department that deals with court martial cases.

We Arora kids—my elder brother, younger sister and I—were petrified of Daddy. Especially me, since I was never really interested in doing well at academics. I believe it was the same with my brother, Chander. It was our sister Kusum who was the studious one. She made up for the juvenile delinquency of her two brothers combined!

Daddy loved hill stations and one of the rare recreational activities that we indulged in as a family, was taking off to picturesque places during our vacations. It was quite a treat for us because thanks to our father's official position, we had access to some special facilities. For example, if we went to colonial-era hill stations such as Ranikhet or Nainital or Kathgodam, we were allowed to stay at the army mess and would also sometimes rent an apartment or book a hotel around these places. We would always carry our bedding, luggage and even cooking utensils in large sacks. My father was not a big fan of eating out every day, so Mummy ji happily handled our holiday kitchen on her own.

In effect, our vacations at hill stations went somewhat like this: wake up, sit together while our mother made breakfast, and then wait for father to summon us with 'Come on, let's get started with studies'. Yes, we would have to study even on vacations!

Over the next few hours, as our mother busied herself in the kitchen, our father would keep us engaged with various math problems while he read the newspapers.

My father loved his long walks. After lunch, he would take us to the forest and show us hidden turns and scenic spots. Sometimes, these walks would go on for hours. In hindsight, it was thanks to our father that we got to explore some truly wonderful hill stations, discover new things to eat, savour and make memories with.

I was curious about everything—it could even be a chicken patty or a nice pastry. I remember on a trip to Mussoorie, I discovered a lovely little bakery next to the army mess and fell in love with their cream rolls. I was very fond of puff pastry and I was so obsessed with the rolls there that I had to have them every day! Today, if someone offers me a cream roll, I may not even touch the creamy, calorie-rich, sinful treat.

I was very fond of playing gully cricket or marbles with my friends. And for as long as I can remember, I had always looked at school as a form of punishment. Being an introverted child, I did not have an active social circle. I always felt shy in a crowd and struggled to answer questions in school or engage with my teachers and classmates freely. I was not articulate at all. I became a laggard because I was too shy, too quiet and too terrified of everything and everyone.

At home, whenever my mother asked me about my day, I had no answer. Mummy ji was not well versed in Math, English, History or Geography, so I used to struggle all by myself, and would occasionally share my problems with my elder brother. If you are lucky, your elder sibling can guide you. In our case, we were both in the same sinking boat!

Over time, with so many girls around me in school, I became more self-conscious. My confidence was tied to my ability to answer correctly when called upon in class. Which rarely happened. Most of the time, I managed to make myself invisible and did not participate actively in the classroom. I struggled with my studies. I hated sports. I hated our physical training (PT) teacher. I felt safe only in my cocoon.

Eventually, I began to skip class, loiter around, play marbles in the gullies and while my time away. My elder brother, who went to the evening school, sometimes caught me in the alleys and promptly ratted me out to my parents. 'Tishi was playing marbles today!' he'd say, calling me by my nickname. And then the usual circus would unfold at home.

When I appeared for my high school final exams, I barely managed to pass. Honestly, I was expecting a second division, but had to contend with a hopeless third.

I remember the day the results came out. In those days, the results were printed in all the newspapers. My father was reading his morning edition when he saw me shuffle around. The conversation was short and hard-hitting, quite literally.

'Result aa gaya?' (Are the results out?)

'Result aa gaya.' (The results are out.)

'Pass ho gaya na?' (Have you passed?)

'Haan ji, pass ho gaya.' (Yes, I have passed.)

'Which division?'

I came up with a bright idea: 'High third division!'

'High third? Woh kya hota hai bakwaas? High ko hawa mein ura do, toh kya bacha? Third!' (What nonsense is that? If the high was to be blown off by the wind, what remains is a shameful third!)

Daddy rolled up his newspaper and . . . *whack!*

But my dismal performance in the school finals was hardly the wake-up call that you would expect it to be. I managed to enrol in an arts degree course at Dyal Singh College—it was obvious that with my kind of grades, I could never become a doctor or an engineer. Neither did I have any inclination to become either of those things. I got bored in just about two weeks of college. That's when a friend came to my rescue and showed me the prospectus of a newly launched catering college in Delhi. Given my serious lack of interest in anything to do with academics, it was no surprise that I had no clue about the Institute of Hotel Management, Catering and Nutrition (abbreviated as IHM) that had come up in Pusa, New Delhi. My friend, who knew how much I liked to eat and of my interest in cooking, opened my eyes to the possibilities of professional education. 'It is a good opportunity,' he said. 'Not only do you learn all about the hospitality industry, you also get to taste good food!'

I was excited. I studied the prospectus closely. With categories such as cookery and baking, it looked extremely tantalising. And yes, the prospect of eating new and different kinds of dishes certainly tipped the scales for me.

Without my father's knowledge, I filled up the form. It was a short and unremarkable form that asked for basic information such as one's father's name and hobbies. There was a bit, however, about why I was keen to join a catering college. My answer was simple, without any artifice: 'Because I love to eat good food, I like to meet people and I like to cook.' Maybe this worked, for shortly after, I received a letter inviting me to appear for an interview. The college was under the aegis of the Ministry of Tourism, Government of India, and seeing the state emblem on the admission letter was a proud moment for me. But when I showed it to my father, he wasn't excited or amused.

Thanks to his work that was mostly in the army headquarters, Daddy was used to the best and brightest in the country—generals and high-ranking civilian officers. His expectations from his sons were high.

In 1963, the concept of celebrity chefs and five-star hotels with their bustling kitchens, was still a rarity. The catering college in Delhi was only a year old and you can imagine Daddy's shock and heartbreak when I showed him the letter and the prospectus.

'Tu bawarchi banega?' (Are you going to become a cook?) he thundered. 'You will ruin my reputation! What are people going to say?'

I was gutted. But somehow, a tiny voice in my head told me that I should try and convince my father. My mother pitched in as well. My father, like so many others of his generation, had little to no knowledge about the hospitality industry, since it was hardly an industry at that time. Anyone who worked in a hotel was either a cook or a waiter. And there was zero respectability attached to either profession, and Daddy was convinced I was perhaps destined to be the latter.

I had twenty days' time to fill the form and deposit my fees. Twenty days to convince my father that given my dismal academic record and my love for food, this was perhaps the best option for me. I was aware of my father's disappointment over my career choice. But I was not aware of how he had already started doing his own homework about the hospitality and catering industry. Through his army sources, he set up an appointment with S.N. Chib, the then Director-General of Tourism.

Mr Chib, who met my father and his colleague, was able to impress upon my father the fact that the government was extremely serious about the tourism and hospitality industry, and how graduates from the catering college could be employed at the many five-star and other prestigious properties of the time. This meeting proved to be a turning point for my father, who then set about helping me get through the interview round. He made me read books and magazines on current affairs, hospitality and catering, and even helped me brush up on my presentation skills. I did my best to convince him that for the first time in my life, I was serious about something!

On the day of the interview, I came face to face with S.N. Chib himself. I was also interviewed by C. Belfield Smith—one of the founding members of the Hotel Catering and Institutional Management Association, United Kingdom, who was assigned to India as an expert by the Food and Agricultural Organization of the United Nations, and was the Principal of IHM in March 1956—and well-known nutritionist, Thangam Philip.

The eminent panel asked me if I had ever stayed or eaten at a five-star hotel.

I answered honestly that the closest I had been to any five-star or upscale eatery or hotel was when I visited Connaught Place (CP). I had never set foot inside any of the famous hotels or restaurants of the time, except for one trip to Moti Mahal in Daryaganj with my family.

I was asked if cooking was a man's job or a woman's. Before you cringe at my response, do remember this was in the 1960s and no one really thought much of a chef, let alone a male one. I answered truthfully: 'It is a woman's job. But I have grown up loving and following my mother's cooking and she is my inspiration behind choosing this as a profession.'

I also told them why I wanted to study catering: 'I love to cook, I love to eat and I love to meet people.'

A few days later, with my admission certificate in hand, Daddy distributed laddoos in the entire neighbourhood. A box was also sent to Mr Chib.

In 1963, IHM was in its second year of existence. There were only fifteen of us in my batch that year. But such was the quality of education that IHM Pusa imparted, that it created some of the future stars of the hospitality business. I remember some of my esteemed colleagues who went on to emerge as industry leaders—my dear friend and exemplary chef the late Chef Arvind Saraswat, and others such as Harish Khanna, Ashok Goyal, Kamal Chopra, Deepak Dutt and Subir Bhowmick, with whom I had the good fortune of working at the Taj as well.

But all my euphoria over getting into IHM disappeared as soon as we found that about the sheer number of subjects we were supposed to study during our course. It was so much more than just cooking—cookery theory, cookery practical, bakery theory, bakery practical, restaurant counter service theory and practical, commodity, law, housekeeping, economics! I was haunted by my academic track record and was anxious not to make a mess of it. At seventeen years,

I was the youngest in my batch. But it helped that I made friends with a bunch of people who were enthusiastic and diligent about the course. It spurred me on.

Some of my closest buddies were Deepak Dutt, Kamal Chopra, Ashok Goel, Rajesh Bhatia and Suresh Khanna. They all hailed from well-heeled and accomplished families.

I was closest to Suresh, who was also my partner at the practical sessions in college. He was a person of few words and was always busy with planning and action. Eventually, the two of us figured out a rhythm for our work, based on our instincts—I used to do most of the actual cooking and Khanna did the planning, cleaning and tidying up after we were done, avoiding wastage, and writing and documenting everything. Eventually, I would also become good friends with Ashok, who was adept at law and accountancy. Over the years, Arvind and Deepak became good friends—there were so many similar bonds that were forged during these golden years that outlasted our time at IHM.

I remember how we decided to bunk college when Arvind's sister was getting married. We wanted to show our support for him by helping out his family. In those days, a daughter's wedding was considered too important and significant to be held anywhere but the family home. I declared that I was going to help out the halwai appointed for catering at the ceremonies. There were six or seven of us in addition to the halwai, who also helped out with the buffet. It was quite a thrill to be able to engage with cooks and halwais as students who were just learning the ropes. We were teenagers, after all, seeking adventure everywhere. But trouble awaited us the next day, when we were barred from attending classes as a punishment for having bunked on the previous day. Word was swiftly sent to our parents and my father, quite uncharacteristically, decided to let me off with a simple reminder of my career prospects!

Those were heady days, indeed. We began to look at every dish and every ingredient in a completely different way, guided by our early knowledge of ingredients, recipes and cooking techniques. Whenever we went out to a restaurant or a party, we would dive into the dishes that we ate, eagerly discussing the taste, texture and guessing what went into the dish and how. When we went to the Marina Hotel (now Radisson Blu Marina Hotel in CP) or the Volga Bar and Restaurant, we would make notes on the ambience, service and food. None of these were five-star properties but popular stand-alone restaurants and hotels—which is all we could afford if we were paying for it!

It was over the course of our many, many foodie adventures that I began to realise how each one of us had a different career plan and passion. Arvind and I were quite similar in the way we visualised our future in the industry. Both of us were passionate about cooking and wanted to be chefs.

And as it so happened, after graduating from college, all of us except for Rajesh Bhatia, joined the Taj Mahal hotel in Mumbai (then Bombay). Arvind, in fact, joined me in the kitchen there, a year later. Deepak Dutt and Kamal Chopra joined the restaurant service at the Taj Hotel and Ashok Goel was put in room service. Harish Khanna and Suresh Khanna had initially joined the Oberoi group of hotels, but later, Harish moved to the Taj. We remained friends and each one of us excelled professionally, rising to prominent positions in the group. In 1973, when I became executive chef, Ashok Goel became room service manager and Arvind became a sous chef at a French restaurant at the Taj, and later on, when the group went on to open a hotel in Chennai in 1980s, he was sent there as executive chef. Meanwhile, Deepak Dutt became a manager at some of our Taj-owned hotels and Kamal Chopra was transferred to Hong Kong to represent the Taj Group at a restaurant there.

But the path to success was not an easy one and it began with us in the first year at IHM. Fond of each other and yet fiercely competitive, each one of us would vie for the attention of our teachers in order to stay ahead of our batchmates. All in good spirit, of course.

For instance, I managed to score a few brownie points with Mrs Krishna Arora, our cookery teacher, who was also our class teacher. It began with me offering to help her prepare for the practical cookery classes—a task that I absolutely loved. Mrs Arora was a legend in her own right. She was a mentor and guide to her students and was also the formulator of the rigorous curriculum that shaped the careers of hundreds of aspirants such as myself. Though she did not treat me any differently than the others, I think she did acknowledge my enthusiasm during the cookery practicals, eventually assigning me the role of class monitor a number of times—a coveted badge for a bunch of teenagers running high on adrenaline.

We spent our first year studying Commodity—the study of all the ingredients used in preparing food—French, Economics, Commerce, Cookery, Bakery and Housekeeping, among other things. But I was only interested in the cookery practical, where we could eat the food that we prepared. After all, this was one of the most important reasons for my joining a catering college. That the course would also give me a professional degree, was another important factor.

Twice a week, we had cookery and bakery classes for almost six hours a day. We were taught the basics, with a focus on continental cuisine, as was the norm in those days. We were introduced to all the primary ingredients and sauces, such as béchamel or white sauce, and we were expected to perfect them. Eventually, we moved on to the first dish of our first year—Chicken a la King. It is a classic and popular continental dish with diced chicken in a cream sauce, often accompanied with sherry, mushrooms and vegetables, and served over rice, noodles or bread. In those days, we did not have the luxury of using red and yellow peppers or any of the other exotic continental vegetables that are so commonplace today. Our Chicken a la King was cooked with capsicum and without sherry.

It was the Chicken a la King challenge that unleashed my competitive streak and gave me the impetus to do better.

Usually, after the cookery teacher's demonstration, the students were divided into seven groups that competed to produce the best version of the dish of the day. One of my classmates was quite the stellar performer during these sessions. The food on her table always looked good, smelled good and tasted divine. Her consistent performance made me wonder—what was holding me back? After all, cooking was something I loved. I gave myself a good kick, and with my partner, Suresh Khanna, took it upon myself to ace all the contests. I began to focus on the ingredients and techniques, pushing myself to perfect everything from preparation to presentation. After six months, when we took our tests, I came out with flying colours—all thanks to my high scores in cookery and bakery. The trend continued right up to my first-year exams, which I cleared with first-class grades. I saw the first hint of pride in my father's smile the day the results came out.

Eventually, it was time for our two-month industrial training that marked the end of the first year. The institute would contact hotel and catering establishments for placements for first-year and second-year students and the Head of the Department at IHM would decide which student got to work where. There was tremendous excitement in the air as we geared up for our first hands-on experience in a proper commercial establishment. I was to work at the legendary Nirula's in Connaught Place, Delhi.

3

Golden Eagle Beer and Béchamel

In the 1960s and 1970s, an opportunity to intern at Nirula's was the magic wand that opened up an exotic and magnificent world of food. It was the first hotel-restaurant set up by Indians in British India with a vow to make European or Western food more accessible to middle-class Indians. The chain traces its origins to the first Hotel India, which was set up in the heart of Delhi's shopping and entertainment district, Connaught Place, in 1934, by brothers L.C. and M. Nirula. Among other things it has a restaurant and a bar.

My first and most lasting memory of Nirula's was the aroma of freshly ground coffee—a novelty in Indian restaurants of the time. It may be difficult for anyone these days to imagine what the smell of coffee did to youngsters growing up in the 1960s, who were so used to sweet masala tea served at roadside stalls or at home. In 1940, on the request of the Indian Coffee Board, Nirula's opened a coffee shop on Janpath and introduced espressos to Indians, sowing the seeds of the vibrant coffee-drinking culture that is so prevalent amongst middle-class Indians today.

The other big draw was the apple strudel, and a trip to Nirula's was always incomplete without it.

Soon afterwards, they launched two themed restaurants—La Boheme, a multi-cuisine restaurant; and Gufa, an Indian restaurant. In the 1950s, they launched Chinese Room, the oldest Chinese restaurant in Delhi.

For the food and beverage (F&B) industry, college students were no more than cheap labour—an extra pair of hands that one could employ wherever, whenever—and no one was interested in teaching interns any tricks of the trade, or sharing any knowledge or experience with them.

I was put to work at the Nirula's pastry and wine shop and for three days, I sold only Golden Eagle beer, which was in huge demand back then. As a young student, who was yet to see the world, it was quite a thrilling experience to sell beer to hundreds of people every day. Even though it was really an innocuous job, I had a strange sense of ownership over it.

But that's where it ended. The managers and other staff would not allow me to go anywhere near the pastries—almost as if my mere presence would ruin them. Maybe they thought I would not be able to do a good job there since there was an astounding variety of pastry items on offer and I did not know the names of half of them. In other words, no one at Nirula's pastry and wine shop took me seriously enough to teach me anything about catering.

Nonetheless, this was when I tasted beer for the first time. I bought a bottle for ₹2 from the shop and shared it with my colleague. Since I was only eighteen years old at the time, I was scared to go home because I didn't want my parents to find out I had been drinking. I managed to sneak home and go straight to bed, without having the usual chat with my parents. I can tell you that I slept soundly that night!

But I was done selling beer. I wanted to be a chef and there was no way I could learn anything if I continued this way. That is when I sneaked into La Boheme. The restaurant had a buzzing dining area and a bustling kitchen that served continental food and some Indian dishes, such as butter chicken and korma. La Boheme's only competition in terms of the food, was Wenger's—a Delhi institution which was more like a coffee shop. La Boheme was no different from the wine and pastry shop. College interns were made to do the dishes, cut and chop vegetables, prep the salad accompaniments, set the tables in the morning and clean the dishes—everything that had nothing to do with either the kitchen or the food.

Most rookies didn't mind this drill. But I was impatient. And after three days, I was done with being treated like menial labour. I realised there was no way I could learn anything here in only two months. I befriended the manager, Pyarelal ji, and mustered the courage to ask for more responsibilities. 'Sir, please can you teach me how to do actual service? I am more interested in the kitchen, but I was sent to the restaurant instead.' Pyarelal smiled and said, 'Don't worry. Work in the restaurant for a month, and I will tell you everything you need to know.'

All my life, I have been lucky to have encountered people who mentored me, helped me, held my hand and guided me at just the right moments. Pyarelal ji turned out to be one such generous soul who took the pains to explain the basics of service in some detail to me.

In college, we had been taught to prepare basic dishes like roast and stewed chicken and lamb, Irish stew, fried fish, baked fish and the likes. But at the restaurant, I saw how a leg of ham was to be carved before guests; how to serve apple sauce, a delicate chicken Milanese, chicken escalope, chicken Bourguignon, fish orly and fish Bonne Femme.

I also saw how the chefs handled the robust Indian dishes, butter chicken, chicken tikka, seekh kebab, and the way they set up kebab platters.

I was hungry for information and hung on to every word uttered by Pyarelal ji, taking down copious notes and going through them at home.

Even though La Boheme's kitchen could accommodate eight people, it still felt fairly small and cramped. I was bewildered to see how it was possible to cater to such a large number of tables from such a small space. After I began to spend more time at the restaurant, I realised how a well-managed kitchen works like a well-oiled machine, how the planning of the kitchen, the layout of the restaurant and the placement of the tables mattered when you wanted smooth service and a bustling, successful restaurant.

After about ten days, Pyarelal ji allowed me to serve one dish and I was kicked! I was an introvert, but I was gradually transforming into a more outgoing person. Service allowed me to interact with the guests, understand what worked and what did not. After serving the guest, I would go back and ask questions: 'How was the food? Did you enjoy it?'

I was not expected to talk to the guests, but I did it because I was genuinely interested in their feedback. Pyarelal ji liked my enthusiasm and began to give me more such opportunities.

Being in the good books of the manager helped me in many other ways as well. Whenever someone left a tip at a table that I had served, Pyarelal ji passed it on to me. It was not the money but his gesture that encouraged me. As I started paying more attention to the tables, I began to earn more and learn more. Sometimes, when people complained about the food, I wanted to understand things better and would nudge them gently for answers. They would perhaps say something vague like, 'The food did not taste that good'. Or sometimes, be a little more specific, like, 'The seasoning was not right'. I watched how the manager handled their feedback. As always, I went home and wrote it all down.

After the first month, I began to nag Pyarelal ji again. 'Sir, please place me in the kitchen now. I want to know how to make spaghetti Bolognese, Chicken a la King and chicken burgers.' Mr Pyarelal had a word with Chef Victor Rodericks about me.

Rodericks was a bit stern at the outset, even intimidating. He bellowed, 'Oye ladke! What will you learn here? You are a skinny fellow. Kitchen work is very heavy, it requires strength.'

I refused to back down. 'No sir, I want to learn.'

Rodericks put me in the vegetable cutting section and I began to learn all about dices, slices, juliennes and more. I was then asked to chop onions and parsley for dishes. Having been brought up in a modest, middle-class home, I had never been exposed to parsley before!

Over time, Rodericks warmed up to me, and I became less nervous about approaching him. He taught me a lot about the different cuts for meats, vegetables, greens and even put me in the roast section, where non-vegetarian continental dishes were cooked.

I wanted to endear myself to the master chef of the section and tried really hard to do so. If there was an order of Chicken a la King, I would run to the fridge and get the chicken pieces and ingredients for the white sauce ready. I observed carefully what happened after the waiter placed the order—the chef would take a pan, add butter and let it melt. He would then add chicken, peppers, a little stock, cream sauce, some seasoning and then send it off. But before that, he would make me taste it. In those days, wine wasn't used for cooking in India. There were a number of reasons behind this. There were no good Indian wines available at that time that would be cost-effective for use in a commercial kitchen. The few good French wines that were integral to French and European cuisine, were prohibitively expensive. Unless you were a celebrity chef and French genius like the famous Rogert Moncourt, who was invited to head the continental kitchen at the Ashoka, Delhi, and could prevail upon the management to procure fine wine for his cooking, it was unheard of.

In dishes where wine was a key ingredient, one could substitute it with more butter, especially for fish fillet, which would dry faster while cooking. Using more butter and cream was also a way to ensure a juicy fish fillet. Some other kitchens would use something called the Vino Royale, which had some alcohol content, but was nothing like the real thing!

Much later, when I eventually joined the Taj, I began to use a bit of wine in some of my French dishes, especially to cater to heads of states such as Francoise Mitterrand. But the Taj was the only hotel, perhaps, that used French wine for cooking French dishes at that time! Eventually, Grover Vineyard began producing affordable Indian wines and we used those.

But this was the mid-1960s and cooks at Nirula's reached for the butter when there was no wine at hand. I also found out that each order of Chicken a la King would taste different. Sometimes, a plate would have too much pepper, another too less, or the white sauce would be inconsistent. There was no standardisation because nothing was by the book and everything was about improvising with whatever ingredients were available to churn up a dish that somewhat resembled the original, but was never quite close. There was no recipe book that told you exactly how much of what you need to prepare a continental classic. How long you must let the white sauce simmer in the pan and to what effect. No wonder then that every time the same chef turned out the same dish, it tasted different. This was a learning for me.

After two months, we returned to college to start our second year. We were asked to make a presentation on all that we had learnt during our field training. I made a chart with my observations under the title 'Restaurant vs Kitchen'. I listed out the problems that the two sections had in coordinating with one another. I had analysed how guests placed their orders, how the orders were written and sent to the kitchen, how the kitchen chef read the orders and shared them with the cooks in his section and how the food was prepared. And since Chicken a la King was so popular, I prepared the dish as a part of my presentation. The principal, Mr Arthur Simms, a British pioneer in catering education, appreciated my work.

In our second year at the catering college, you can say I struck gold—we were taught all about Indian cuisine, my favourite.

We were taught everything we needed to know about Indian spices and herbs. Most of us were familiar with the ingredients at home, but now we were taught how to look at every element minutely. What jeera or cumin seeds looked like, when haldi or turmeric should be added to a dish, the fragrance and colour of pure dhaniya or coriander powder.

I teamed up with my old pal Suresh Khanna for the cooking practical, and the two of us put together dishes that would reflect who we were, our story and our culinary experience. Growing up, we had both made frequent trips to the famous Gulati or Pindi restaurants on Pandara Road, well-loved for their typical North Indian fare. We remembered how the chefs there would stress on 'bhunna'—the North Indian technique of frying the masala and the ingredients well enough to bring out the flavours of the dish. And we attempted to replicate the same process. Suresh and I worked beautifully as a team, sometimes preparing dishes together, and at other times, taking turns to do the mise en place and bringing together the final elements of the dish at the table in front of the guest.

But with all our focus on the dishing out bit, we did not pay attention to how we were actually overdoing the spices. More importantly, we had no idea of the right sequence. We did not know that one first had to heat the cooking medium, then pop the dry whole spices because Indian spices are porous, and then add the onions, followed by the meat or vegetables. We just wanted to reach the finishing line, hoping that the end would justify the means. So we were almost always working backwards, trying to replicate the final texture, colour and aroma, while being oblivious to something as crucial as roasting the spices well before frying the meat.

We may not have fared too well at the test, but we learned from our mistakes. The exposure to the finer nuances of Indian cuisine at IHM, despite all the wonderful French and Italian and Mexican food that we had been taught to prepare, convinced me that I wanted to be a professional chef. I knew how to make a fine chicken stew, but I was a Punjabi boy in love with and inspired by his mother's cooking. The music of a spicy tadka in hot oil was sweeter than a classical symphony to my ears.

I also began to interact with my teachers and fellow students a lot more and it lent a certain spring to my step. I did exceedingly well in my second year and, as a reward, was sent to intern at The Oberoi Grand in Calcutta, my first five-star experience. The hotel had an impeccable legacy and was a favourite with the most elegant travellers of the time. It had 300 rooms, Indian, French and Chinese restaurants, two coffee shops, a lounge, a bar and banquet rooms.

The main kitchen was massive. Mr Bose was the executive chef and was extremely helpful towards his staff and young college students. After a brief interaction with me, he understood I wanted to be a chef and chalked out a training programme for me in the kitchen. Butchery for three days, vegetable cutting for three days, roast section for three weeks—which was where the continental food was prepared—Indian food for three weeks and the banquet kitchen for one week. At the end of each module, he would take feedback from the various section heads and from the interns, to understand how things were progressing.

In butchery, we were taught how to cut meat and fish according to the dish, and in a separate section, we learned all about cutting vegetables—batons, slices, brunoise. The third is a culinary knife cut in which the vegetable is first julienned and then gathered into strips together and turned at a 90 degree angle and diced again, producing cubes of about 3 millimetres (1/8 inches) or less on each side.

In the roast section, I learned how to make the mother sauces—veloute, béchamel, hollandaise, tomato sauce and Espagnole—as well as brown gravy and tomato-based gravy. I took notes at each step for all the recipes. I also learned how to handle beef fillets, lamb chops and make a variety of soups, including mushroom, mulligatawny, tomato, minestrone, water cress.

My shifts were 9 AM to 3 PM and 6 PM to 12 midnight, but my mind was on fire and I wanted to see more, learn more and do more. I started going in at 7 AM because I did not want to miss breakfast service, and would stay on till 1 AM for the coffee shop. In between, I would make time for the banquet kitchen as well.

My days at the Oberoi Grand were not all smooth sailing, though—in a bustling five-star kitchen, tempers are bound to rise. And sometimes, I would make novice mistakes that would trigger the professionals. Despite my enthusiasm and eagerness to learn, I was still, obviously, pretty wet behind the ears.

Once, I was cooking chicken stroganoff and I put sour cream in a pan on high flame. It curdled immediately. Chef Chatterjee, who was taking care of that dish, lost his cool. However, while reprimanding me soundly for what I had done, he also made it a point to let me know the correct way to do it. 'Don't you know cream curdles on a high flame? You should add it very slowly and mix it well, gradually, with the sauce and make sure you are not cooking on a high flame,' he said while demonstrating the process. And then, while grilling prawns on the grill one day, I forgot to regulate the heat—so much so that all the prawns turned rubbery. The day I was cooking lobster Thermidor, I didn't realise that brandy burns so quickly, and ended up with a disaster of a dish. The professional chefs, at every point—despite my many rookie mistakes—made the effort to not simply reprimand me but also teach me how exactly it was to be done. How one had to keep removing the prawns from the grill and touch the pieces to check if they were underdone or cooked all the way through. What was the point at which brandy would begin to burn and how never to lose your nerve in the kitchen, even when you have an accident.

Of all the modules, however, it was in the Indian section where I felt truly at home. Traditional Indian dishes such as Chicken Makhani, korma, Rogan Josh, were not something we got to make every day at the institute. I was still in the early stages of learning then, and as much as I loved Indian food, I was apprehensive about approaching it—I found it somewhat messy and complicated, compared to the continental dishes that we had grown used to making. Also, there was no concept of serving Indian food in a fine-dining setup at the time; it was mostly all dumped in a bowl and not really plated as elegantly as continental or French food. The Oberoi changed all that for me. While food was not plated, they served it in elegant silver salvers and garnished every dish with vegetables and herbs to make them look enticing. In the kitchen, I learned the fine art of dicing and chopping.

Ustad Dhani Ram, the head chef of the Indian section, showed me how to slide the knife through a chunk of onion while sliding it down your finger as well, to avoid injuring yourself. At the institute, we had once made Rogan Josh, but the lamb had turned out chewy. Ustad Dhani Ram showed me how you could use kachri, a kind of nutmeg, to ensure that your lamb cooked faster and became so tender that it slid off the bone.

He showed me how to add milk to pulao to lend it a brilliant white colour. And how to add roasted besan to chicken tikka in case you did not have cashew nut paste, to make the tikkas softer and tastier. Once you coated the tikka in besan, the yogurt would stick to the pieces easily and your tikka would be nicely browned and bursting with flavour. It was food alchemy at its most elegant.

The Oberoi was also where I got a taste of what a refined work culture in the hospitality business was really like. I was still a teenager but they were as keen to teach me as I was to learn. They treated me at par and even allowed me to be present at the tables sometimes when food was served and the chef conversed with the guests, dressed in chef whites. It was an honour and I got a taste of belonging to the clan, so to speak. It was an experience that stayed with me and even today, when I make Rogan Josh or Chicken Makhani, there is a part of my mind that goes back to my days at the Oberoi.

By the time I returned to college to begin my third year, there were only ten of us left as some students had dropped out to pursue other career options. I worked hard on my presentation and the new principal, Mr Achyutan Menon, was impressed enough with my work to award me a merit certificate. What's more, I was asked to be the monitor during all cookery classes. It was nothing short of a jackpot for a novice like me.

Our third year was special—we had the chance to learn from the aforementioned noted French chef, Roger Moncourt, who worked at The Ashoka Hotel in Delhi.

The Ashoka Hotel, a cultural and hospitality icon that was established by our first Prime Minister Shri Jawaharlal Nehru, was where royalty, aristocrats, heads of state and diplomats socialised. The hotel was most popular during the 1960s and 1970s, and often hosted live performances by the country's top artists and grand state buffets for political VIPs. It was to Delhi's power circles what the Taj was to Bombay's business elite. The high-profile hotel was also where you could sample the finest international cuisine. Its French restaurant Rougenoire, which had a glamorous nightclub-like ambience, served the classiest French cuisine in town, thanks to Chef Roger Moncourt. Pandit Nehru had invited Chef Moncourt to India and tasked him with introducing elite Indians to the nuances of French cuisine. Chef Moncourt quickly attained a cult following among gourmands and aspiring chefs for creating popular signature desserts at The Ashoka, such as the Bombé Ashoka—vanilla ice cream topped with rum-soaked raisins and chocolate flakes.

Twice a week, Chef Moncourt used to host a workshop with us at IHM. And twice a week, I would be transported to a fantasy world where the most exotic, classiest and finest culinary techniques, tricks and treats would be revealed to us. Chef Moncourt was a master of haute cuisine and had an astounding grip on the grammar of classical French cuisine. He showed us techniques such as braising, basting and sweating. It was thanks to him that we learnt how different kinds of knives were used for different cuts. He was extremely particular about his own set—much like an artist about his paintbrushes. Chef Moncourt shared many stories of his life in France with us, and I realised just how much respect Europeans treated chefs with. They were treated as if they were artists—a far cry from the dismissive and derogatory treatment that we were subjected to in our country. Being called a 'bawarchi' was an abuse and had none of the respectability that the 'chef' tag carried in the First World.

Now, if one is really interested in cooking, one would want to see what happens in the pan when an ingredient is 'sweating', or how to braise a joint. In other countries, demonstration kitchens are fitted with a mirror right above the chef, so that anyone standing behind him can get a clear view of what was happening in the pan. However, in India, back in the mid-1960s, there were no mirrors or proper demonstration kitchens. Added to this was the fact that I was short, so I couldn't see anything if I stood too far behind the chef. And I desperately wanted to watch Chef Moncourt cook. So whenever he held his workshop, I would quickly take my place right in the front. As soon as he announced the dish of the day, I would volunteer to chop the onions or do something to help him, so that I could get a better view of the pan.

After this happened a few times, I started being called a sycophant, a chamcha. But it didn't matter to me. I was hungry for knowledge and I wanted to learn everything—the temperature at which wine becomes vinegar, for example. I knew every small detail would matter if I wanted to become a professional chef.

We had to specialise in one field in our fourth and final year, and I opted for kitchen planning—how to choose the right location and the right property; how to plan the kitchen's layout; study the neighbourhood and the target audience. Meanwhile, Moncourt was to teach us advanced French and Italian cooking. We learned how to make chicken chasseur, Derby chicken, fillet of pomfret Bonne Femme, the regular fish and chips, Chicken a la Kiev, lasagna, minestrone soup, etc. We were also taught how to prepare basic hot French and Italian sauces like béchamel, veloute and Espagnole, and cold sauces such as hollandaise, mayonnaise and their derivatives: Mornay, suprême, demi-glace and aioli. We also had classes on how to plan a kitchen. It was a challenging and fulfilling year for us.

My rapport with Moncourt extended beyond the time he spent teaching us at IHM. I must say my internship at the Oberoi, where I was exposed to the basics of continental cooking, played a part. At times, on Sundays, I used to go Ashoka Hotel to work with him in his kitchen, where he used to put me with his chefs, who would assign me small tasks like cutting vegetables, roasting potatoes and other vegetables, making mashed potato. These may seem like menial tasks, but the experience bolstered my confidence to a great extent. After all, I was spending invaluable time in another five-star kitchen, working with a team headed by a world-renowned chef!

I would like to think I made an impression on Mr Moncourt, because when we finished our course, he invited me to join the kitchens of The Ashoka Hotel. He also told me I was one of his best students. As grateful as I was to Mr Moncourt, and despite the fact that the Ashoka was a glittering showpiece for the government that was in line to put India on the global tourism and hospitality map, my heart was not quite in pursuing a career there. To be fair, the Ashoka attracted the top dignitaries of Delhi at the time and whenever I visited Moncourt, I would see him attending to a banquet or an event where he would be dressing lavish plates with continental and French delicacies. I knew by refusing to work in that environment where I could learn and grow as a continental chef under my highly accomplished mentor, I risked losing a friend for life.

But I also knew that the Tatas had enviable business ethics and were better employers than the government. Besides, I dreamed of working with not a state icon, but an industry icon in hospitality. And then, as luck would have it, I got an offer that I could not refuse. A decision that changed my life forever.

4

All Roads Lead to the Taj

Ever since I had become serious about my career as a chef, I had dreamed of working at the Taj Hotel some day. In the 1960s, the Tata Group had not ventured into the hospitality business beyond their iconic Bombay property. And for an entire generation of Indians, the Taj Hotel was the ultimate symbol of refinement, glamour, elegance and hospitality, and was synonymous with the spirit of Bombay.

This desire was not just triggered by the grandeur of the architecture and the remarkable story behind the creation of the property, which had risen in majestic defiance against the British, who had once snubbed Mr Jamsetji Tata at a hotel in Europe. The Taj represented Indian pride and had a work culture that is exemplary. I had heard only the best things about the Tata group and the way they nurtured talent. All the magazines I had read about the hospitality business, all the discussions I had heard among chefs and everything I had seen or heard elsewhere had created this impression in my mind—the Taj Mahal hotel was the holy grail of the hospitality industry.

Buoyed by my first-class degree and excellent grades in my favourite subjects—cookery and bakery—I applied for a position in the kitchen at the Taj, among other places. I was plucky, but I had nothing to lose. I got a call from the Taj, but they offered me the position of an order-taker for room service. I wrote back to them, simply saying that I wanted to join the kitchen. Call it my audacity or confidence, but my courage paid off.

For the first round of interviews, I was asked to show up at the Tata House in Connaught Place, where I faced Mr Jagat Verma, who was sous chef at that time, Food and Beverage Manager Mr N.B. Daruwala, Personnel Manager Chitra Bali and Mr Karve, the administrator.

Mr Daruwala asked me directly: 'Why do you want to join the Taj kitchen?'

'Sir, most of my industrial training has been in commercial kitchens, including the Oberoi Grand. And I have always wanted to be a chef,' I said frankly.

But it seemed to go downhill from thereon because the panel was not convinced—given my small frame—that I would survive the long hours in a busy five-star kitchen. I was firm in my replies, talking about all the extra hours I had put in with Moncourt and the Ashoka, but all that the Taj panel was willing to offer me was a position in room service. They even grilled me on why I had not taken up the offer to join Ashoka.

At every step, I held my ground. I reiterated my ambition to become a chef and work with the Taj Mahal Hotel. I could sense they were somewhere between a 'yes' and a 'no'.

I walked out of Tata House feeling anxious—they wanted two weeks to think it over.

Those two weeks were perhaps the longest of my life. I was wondering if I had done the right thing by turning down the ridiculously good offer from Moncourt and taking a chance on the Taj instead. After two nail-biting weeks, I got a letter. They seemed to be somewhat convinced and called me for an interview with the venerable General Manager (GM) Mr Ajit Kerkar in Bombay.

I met Mr Kerkar—a man who had shaped the destinies of so many talented chefs over the decades and who was instrumental in giving the Taj Hotel its identity. The interview turned out to be an interesting one. I was asked to name some Indian dishes and some continental ones, and was asked to plan a menu for ten people in the continental style.

I replied, 'I would make a prawn cocktail, a chicken in red wine sauce, where I will stuff the chicken breast with spinach and cheese and then cook it in red wine sauce. I will use vegetables like rose potato and carrots as a side. I will make a chocolate mousse or a caramel custard—simple but delicious, just like the way we have learned.'

This session marked the end of the first round. For my second round of interviews in Bombay, I found myself in Mr Kerkar's office with Chitra Bali, N.B. Daruwala and the same panel as before.

Mr Kerkar began on a serious note. 'My colleagues tell me that you are adamant on joining the kitchen. Why?'

I was ready with my answer. 'Sir, when I joined catering college, I knew that my life would be all about working with food. I have always been very fond of eating food and from eight years of age, I have been helping my mother out in the kitchen—'

Mr Kerkar interrupted me, 'Your mother's kitchen is a home kitchen. Do you think you will be able to survive in a kitchen that caters to a five-star hotel with 300 rooms?'

I knew I was being tested severely but I was determined not to give up. 'Please give me a chance, sir. If at any point I let you down, I will resign and go back to Delhi.' To be honest, in the back of my mind, I already knew I had a Plan B—Ashoka and Moncourt.

Kerkar continued, 'But then you will have to do long hours.'

'Yes sir, I will do long hours.'

'Do you have accommodations in Bombay?'

'No sir, but I will search.'

'Do you know how difficult it is to find one?'

'Sir, if I have decided to make a career in this city, I will definitely find one.'

Maybe I came across as a bit too confident and Kerkar decided to test me again. 'Do you know anything at all about kitchen planning?'

That's when all the training we had received in the fourth year came to my aid. Mr Kerkar gave me a piece of paper and told me to plan a kitchen for a restaurant which could accommodate 100 people. He was about to start another meeting and before I could begin, I asked him a few questions—what kind of cuisine would be served; was it a fine-dining restaurant or a casual one? I also asked if any live cooking was expected to be done.

He looked pleasantly surprised. 'Oh! Do those details matter?'

I replied, 'Yes sir, they do matter.'

Mr Kerkar was probably testing me at that point. He told me to make a rough plan for a fine-dining restaurant. We had been taught motion studies, which included accommodating details like the distance waiters needed to walk so that they wouldn't get tired carrying the heavy trays of food, and whether the entrance and exit to the kitchen were to be different or not. Keeping all these things in mind, I explained my plan to him.

After I finished, he paused for a few seconds before he uttered the words that would change my life forever.

'Issue him a letter. He should join as a trainee chef,' he said to the personnel manager.

Words cannot describe my feelings at that time as I fought hard to hold back my tears of pure joy. He asked me when I could join and I said that I needed a week's time to sort everything out. And that was it. I was on the path to my dream destination—Taj Bombay.

My father was delighted. His slacker of a son had finally redeemed himself. I was twenty years old and would be going to live away from home for the first time—for my dream job. He was aware of the respect that Taj Hotel commanded and was proud of my achievements. I could see it in his eyes. We celebrated by going out for a family dinner to a modest but buzzing restaurant called Shiv Sagar.

Throughout college, I would come home and tell my mother about all the cooking that I had done that day. She would greet me with a smile, but I had a feeling that she wondered why a boy from a family of government job holders, who could be a doctor or an engineer or something along those lines, wanted to be a chef in a kitchen. Her smile of bewilderment changed into one of pride and happiness when I landed my dream job at the Taj. I could see that spark in her eyes that said: 'I'm proud of you, my naughty one!'

---

11 September 1967. It has been more than five decades since I first stepped into the Taj Hotel; my shrine, my karma

bhoomi. But I can recall my first day there in vivid detail, even today.

As trainees, all of us had to undergo a week-long induction programme. If someone was supposed to join the kitchen, they could start only after having worked in the other departments in order to gain a better understanding of the entire chain—purchases, the restaurant, housekeeping. The day I joined the Taj, there was a major function where V.V. Giri, president of India, was the chief guest. It was a tea party and six of us trainees were asked to work the banquet. The manager told us to clean the glasses until they were spotless and sparkling. There were 500 guests in attendance and so there were a lot of glasses!

We scrubbed, cleaned, polished till 1 PM, yet nobody asked us to go for our lunch break. Being trainees, we had no courage to tell the manager that we were dying of hunger, and kept cleaning the glasses till 3 PM. As soon as we were done with the last of the 500 pieces, we were given a fresh set of chores that kept us busy till 5 PM. It was time for the president to arrive and nobody had any time or bandwidth to deal with us.

The event finally got over at 6:30 PM and everyone left without even as much as acknowledging the effort we had put in. Hungry, tired and a little angry, a fellow trainee and I found some extra coconut macaroons on the banquet table, which we stuffed into our pockets and walked out. We sat at the Gateway of India, the most famous landmark of Bombay, which stands in front of the hotel, and silently devoured our first morsel of food since the morning. The concrete benches facing the Arabian Sea felt cold, hard and unfriendly. The majestic hotel seemed indifferent to us.

I remember feeling disappointed with the way we had been treated on our first day. The euphoria and excitement of having landed my dream job disappeared. What remained was the feeling that no one cared about us.

But I was soon going to be proven wrong.

5

'Prawns Chheela'

After one week, I was finally allowed to step into the kitchen. The executive chef at that time was an old Goan gentleman called Mr Mascarenhas. I consider him to be one of my gurus now, but on that first day, I felt rather intimidated by him. He made me wait outside his office after I showed up to work, while he went around yelling instructions at other members of staff.

Mascarenhas kept going in and out of his cabin, without even looking at me. Eventually, I approached someone who was wearing a chef's uniform. Having watched him bustle around the kitchen, I assumed he was the sous chef. I was hungry and asked him if I could go have lunch.

He looked at me curiously and said, 'Who are you and why have you come here?'

It was only then that I realised nobody knew anything about my being there. I introduced myself politely and got his permission to go for lunch. I returned and reclaimed my position outside the executive chef's office once again, and stayed put till 5:30 PM. All the while, not a single person had spoken to me. When it was time to go home, the sous chef asked me to come back the next day.

I was upset. What kind of an induction was this, I wondered? But I shook off my misgivings. 'No matter how tough they make it for me, I will stick around here,' I told myself.

The two experiences, one at the president's tea party and the other in the kitchen, stayed with me till the time I was put in charge of the kitchen as the executive chef. To ensure that no trainee goes through the humiliation we were inadvertently subjected to and form an unfavourable impression of the Taj, I created a buddy system in the kitchen where every trainee would be assigned a senior kitchen staff member, who would help them find their way around the systems and processes. I also created a detailed induction programme so that trainees did not waste any time waiting outside office doors simply to get noticed.

You see, in 1973, when I became the executive chef, and even later, I felt that it was quite difficult to get trained chefs in our industry. In the 1980s, particularly, chefs had started going abroad to Dubai, other Middle-Eastern countries and Europe, after which began the exodus to Australia. This left a huge talent void in our kitchens. So we developed a training programme with a panel comprising a chef (which was me), food and beverage manager, and someone from the human resources (HR) department. We started campus recruitment for the first time. We started visiting catering colleges to interview students directly, who were due to graduate soon, during their third year. We devised a training programme for three years.

For this, I even involved my senior sous chefs to take care of the new inductees. We interviewed students when they came to the Taj. They were first rotated between allied departments—like purchase, banquet office, F&B, cost control, goods receiving, room service—for a period of fifteen days. This was followed by a day-long induction programme, where they were briefed about the hotel and shown a video introducing them to the senior staff and departments connected to food production.

I would then attach the trainees to different sections of the main kitchen, like butchery, cold kitchen, bakery, confectionery, breakfast section, Indian section, continental section—which was further divided into roast section, fresh section, vegetable section, Indian non-veg, Indian vegetarian, Tandoori etc. The two-year programme was monitored by my sous chefs and guided by department chefs. For the buddy system, I put three chefs to take care of the new joinees. I would leave them with the instruction, 'If you have any problem, go to this chef. Don't go here and there. This is the chef who will liaison with me or sous chefs, and try to solve all your problems.'

I used to conduct theory classes twice a week and every month, would seek a report from each of the departments where the new joinees were working. After two years of training, gauging their interest levels and skills, combined with inputs from their sectional heads, I would assign them sections for the rest of their tenure. For example, if someone did well in the Indian or banquet section, I would assign them to the Indian restaurant or in banqueting. It was a simple but streamlined process.

This way, I thought, we could help young chefs develop their skills based on their aptitude. In the final six months of their training, the trainee chefs were sent to the various Taj properties in Delhi, Bangalore, Madras and Calcutta, based on their performance in their respective sections in Bombay. And that's how, by the end of two and a half years, I used to get a team of well-trained chefs.

I have been lucky to have trained some young chefs through this programme, who went on to carve out successful career trajectories for themselves in India and abroad. Cyrus Todiwala, Sriram Aiylur, K. Natarajan, Vikram Sundaram, to name a few, are still very close to me.

Back in the early days of my working at this kitchen, things somehow moved on the next day and the personnel department finally introduced me to Mr Mascarenhas formally. The sous chef placed me in the butchery department to start off. I found a chef's coat that was a few sizes too big for my slight frame, and walked in, bright as day. But my happiness at having found a toehold in the kitchen was short-lived.

I was supposed to work under the formidable butcher who used to handle the fish and seafood section. He was called Boxer—no one knew his real name. The first thing he did was hand over 50 kilos of prawns to me and said, 'Peel them, son'.

I staggered under the enormity of the task, gulped nervously, mustered all my humility and said, 'Sir, could you please tell me how to do it?'

Boxer smirked. 'You have graduated from a catering college, haven't you? And you don't know how to shell prawns?'

And with that slap on my confidence, I was left alone with 50 kilos of prawns that had to be shelled and cleaned, poop chute and all.

It is important to remember that almost everyone working in commercial kitchens at that time had learned on the job. Boxer was no different. Many senior people in the kitchen had been around for years and took considerable pride in being self-taught, and in their ability to have survived and succeeded in high-pressure, high-profile kitchens. It was perhaps natural for them to look at farm-fresh youngsters from newly established catering colleges with resentment. We seemed to make seemingly easy debuts in the fiercely competitive and tough spaces that they had fought hard to enter. A lot of the bitterness that one faced early on came from a place of insecurity and a lack of awareness on the part of the veterans.

The hospitality industry was changing at a furious pace and we were part of the change. This also entailed facing resistance from the old order. It happens in every kitchen and even in every home. When a younger, more aware and modern person starts getting involved in the kitchen, there is bound to be friction from the family matriarch or the homemaker who is used to exercising unquestioned authority over the space that they may have built from scratch. The Taj was no different.

I knew I was being ragged. Tested. People were cynical about my ability to survive in the kitchen and were bound to do everything to make it difficult for me. They were waiting for me to drop my apron and run out. But I was one hell of a tough cookie.

Cleaning the 50 kilos of prawns took up almost the entire day. But I did not stop till I was done. When I went home, I felt a sharp, searing pain in my right thumb and fingers. I could not sleep that night as the pain intensified and I came down with high fever. I realised, to my horror, that the shells of the prawns had injured my skin and the minute wounds had contracted septic.

I was completely gutted. How could I go back to the hotel the next day and tell Mr Jagat Verma, the sous chef, that I had wounded myself on my first day in the kitchen? Would they throw me out? Would this be the end of my career? I tossed and turned all night, burning up with fever and anxiety.

The next morning, I gathered all my courage and walked up to Mr Verma. I told him about what had happened and he immediately sent me to the resident doctor, who reprimanded me for not having come in for a tetanus shot earlier. Shots taken, I was asked to rest at home for the next few days.

After three days, I reported back to work. This time, I was standing in front of the executive chef.

'Kya karne ko aaya tum idhar? (What have you come here for?),' he bellowed.

'Sir, I'm a trainee chef.'

'Kya kiya abhi tak? (What have you done so far?)'

'Prawns chheela!' I was aware my accomplishments were miniscule.

'What did you do after that?'

'Sir, I fell ill,' I said embarrassed.

Mr Verma dismissed me off-handishly. 'Oh, so you cannot work in the kitchen!'

I immediately started begging and pleading, pride be damned! 'Sir, please don't say that. I will do whatever you ask me to.'

He finally relented and sent me to the sous chef again. This time, I was asked to peel my way through an entire sack of onions. I started bravely, but soon tears were rolling down my face. In college, I had peeled onions, but not 50 kilos at once. Next, I was placed in the vegetable section, where the chef gave me tons of vegetables to peel for the Indian and continental dishes that the chefs were preparing.

Slowly, I got into my old habit of maintaining a logbook and noting down all that I had done, seen and learned. I began to gain confidence, learning from the formidable chefs around me. Though my work hours were from nine to five, I would stay on till closing time, much later in the evening. I did not have anyone to go back home to, and I did not quite fancy roaming around the city. The Taj kitchen was the only world I cared to know better. It was the only world I wanted to belong in.

Bombay in 1967 was a very different city from what Mumbai is today. It wasn't as crowded or polluted. Transportation was smooth and the iconic black-and-yellow Premier Padmini taxis were easily available. There are still certain things that have not changed over the decades. Especially for out-of-towners such as myself. Finding a decent place to stay is as much a challenge today as it was at that time. It is quite strange, really. The city can be so generous at one level, giving you innumerable opportunities and exposure. And yet, it has always been one of the toughest places to find a roof over your head.

For my first week in Bombay, I stayed at my friend Ashok Goel's place, a few lanes away from the Taj. It was a 15x15 feet room, in an old building that belonged to the Port Trust. Each floor had six or seven such rooms and a common toilet. Ashok was a classmate of mine from catering college and agreed to share his single PG room with me after he found out I had failed to find decent accommodation in the city. This sort of subletting or sharing was against the housing society rules and we had to plan an elaborate cat-and-mouse game in order to not get caught.

Most evenings, after wrapping up my work at the Taj, I would sneak back into the room under the cover of night and return to the hotel at 6 AM. It was not a dignified thing to do, but I didn't have a choice. After a week, the landlord caught me sneaking in. My friend tried to cover for me, introducing me as a relative, and the PG owner agreed to let me sleep in the room at night, but laid down one condition—there would be no space provided for my luggage. What little I owned did not take up a lot of space, but neither of us had the luxury to argue with him. So the next day, after getting barely any sleep in my friend's tenement, I went to Bombay Central Station, used the cloakroom to store my luggage and took a shower in the railways toilet before going to the hotel. That's how I lived for the next three days.

It was around this time that someone suggested a guest house located not far from the Taj, where I could rent a room with three other people. For ₹375, we would get three beds in a room, with a cupboard and common toilets shared between six people. I roped in two friends to share the room with me, and promptly moved in.

My extra hours at the Taj helped me make more friends and eventually, the chef put me in the roast section for three months, followed by the fish section for another three months. Given the scale at which the Taj functioned, there were several parties every day with a thousand portions of roasted meat being used for the various dishes. And given that continental food was the top choice for banquets and the buffet spreads, the roast and the fish sections were the backbones of the kitchen.

At that time, the Taj kitchen used only oil-fired ranges. They didn't have sophisticated gas ranges and one ended up sweating profusely while working with the traditional ranges. I had to take a long shower as soon as I finished work. My health was not in top form, but my mind was on fire. And that's how my journey started—in the rough and tumble of the kitchen that catered to the world. I simply kept my head down and worked my way through every step, spending more and more time in the kitchen, so that one day, I could make my way around it blindfolded.

At that time, the Taj was paying me stipend of ₹350 a month. To put things in perspective, a bottle of Coke at that time cost only 50 paise. The hotel provided us with food and water, so earning that kind of money was a luxury for me. I lived frugally, but I remember vividly how I spent my first salary.

I watched a movie starring my favourite Hindi filmstar, Mumtaz. Therafter, I had a decadent meal at Bade Miyaan, a landmark street-food joint which is popular for its Mughlai dishes such as baida roti (a deep-fried egg and Indian flat bread dish), seekh kebab, mutton tikka and Bhuna Chicken. Over the next few weeks, I watched the Mumtaz movie three more times. Little did I know that someday, I would prepare a grand feast for her wedding!

After six months, Mr Kerkar, the GM, called me and said, 'I find you to have the makings of a good chef. We have decided to send you for training to Germany for a year.'

I stared at him—I didn't know how to thank him. This was the ultimate fantasy for a middle-class Punjabi boy like me. It would be my first time on a plane. I had no clue what an airplane even looked like from the inside! I had taken a train from Delhi, after all.

I thanked him and walked out, with fresh determination to work even harder and make everyone proud of the little trainee chef who had fallen sick after peeling prawns on his first day!

6

Thirty-Two Dishes for Mr Kerkar

Finally in July 1968, I was to leave for my training at the Park Hotel, Dusseldorf, and at Hotel Frankfurter Hof, Frankfurt—both part of the Steigenberger Hotels and Resorts group. I was to stay in Germany for a full year. For someone who had never seen the inside of an airplane, the flight to Germany was terrifying. It was a long, eight-hour flight. And I tried to control my anxiety by focusing on the food that was served—omelettes and casseroles.

My anxiety disappeared as soon as we landed. I felt better when I saw that someone had come to pick me up. I was to stay in a neat one-bedroom apartment. After the pigeonholes of Bombay, it was a welcome change. I was happy with the way the staff welcomed me and made me feel comfortable. Later, I was introduced to everyone at the Park Hotel kitchen as 'the boy from the Taj Mahal Hotel who is here for training'. And that's how a new chapter in my life began unfolding.

During my training, the director of the hotel, Mr Teal Winkler, watched me like a hawk. I was determined to impress him and wanted to learn as much as possible. I had a single-minded focus—I wanted to become a chef that the Taj would be proud of.

I was also dealing with my personal problems, mostly to do with my food habits. German cuisine features an abundance of beef and pork, which I do not eat. Back in those days, there were no Indian restaurants in Dusseldorf either. So on the pretext of introducing the kitchen staff to Indian cuisine, I began putting together things that I could eat.

But before I could make my colleagues and hosts eat my kind of food, I had to talk their talk. I began to hang around when kitchen orders were received, to pick up words and phrases. I learnt that kartoffel is potato, essen is a meal. Junger mann is young man. I had also done preliminary homework on greetings and other social customs before leaving. But the best way to make friends in a new culture is by sharing food. There was a custom of the staff eating together around noon before the restaurant commenced lunch service. We would gather in the chef's dining room to chat and eat—I used these moments to present my Indian dishes to them.

One day, I made a simple chicken curry and asked them to taste it. The executive chef liked it very much, though he thought it was a little spicy. I promised to make him something else next time. My second attempt was a mild lamb korma, served with some rice. The kitchen staff loved it and asked me many questions about how I had achieved the tenderness in the meat and what went into the gravy, since they were tasting something like it for the first time. I explained how I had marinated the lamb first for half an hour, then I poached it in stock. I then removed the lamb and made a creamy sauce with cashew paste and immersed the lamb in it. They were left wide-eyed—this was their first brush with Indian cooking and they admitted they had no idea that it involved such a laborious process.

These little food adventures not only helped me strike a rapport with the team, but also helped me eat better. Soon, my friends at the kitchen began to look forward to lunchtime so they could taste some of the Indian dishes that I cooked. Everything was a novelty for them, and familiar comfort for me.

My exposure and training in continental cuisine continued at the group's other property, Frankfurter Hof, in Frankfurt, which was popular for its banquet facilities. The chefs there had heard about my Indian dishes and wanted me to show them a few things about our techniques and spices. In turn, they were generous with their knowledge and skill. I learnt new and complex dishes there. At times, I was even left alone in the kitchen, which added to my confidence.

In Dusseldorf and now in Frankfurt, I experienced what global kitchens were actually like. Not only was I handling far superior kitchen equipment, I was working with better ingredients as well. At least better than what one was used to in India's top five-star hotel in the late 1960s. For example, the Taj used to import broccoli from Holland—it was not grown in India at that time and hence we always had to use it in frozen form. While we were used to using dried rosemary, thyme and other herbs in India, in Germany we were using fresh herbs with the best wines to make the most flavourful stock. Even something as commonplace these days as bell peppers were not available, and I actually got to use them in my cooking for the first time in Germany. I was like a child in a candy shop!

During my Frankfurt stint, I also learned the basics of banquet planning. More than half their parties were sit-down formal dinners with at least three courses that required meticulous planning. I was working with the chef responsible for banquets and I watched him plan the menu in great detail, working out the exact quantity of fish, meat, vegetables and fruits required for the events and work out pre-prep time and cooking time and serving time down to the last fraction. This study would eventually go on to help me during my days at the Taj afterwards, while handling some of the most famous banquets for heads of states and Bollywood A-listers.

The months went by just like that, immersed in the world of glorious food, learning from global experts and catering to a very discerning and different kind of Western palate. The training opened my mind. When I was due to return to India, the director praised my performance and offered me a position at the hotel in Germany, which I politely declined.

'Sir,' I said, respectfully, 'I have a professional and ethical commitment to the Taj, since they have sent me here, and I cannot betray their trust. But I do have an elder brother who has recently graduated from catering college. Maybe you can consider him instead.'

After dragging himself through Dyal Singh College, Delhi University, my elder brother, Chander, had managed to convince my father that there was no future in the academic degree he was pursuing and had joined the Pusa catering college instead. When I had fifteen days left in Germany, I used the time to help my brother secure a work permit. He flew down immediately and joined their kitchen. Chander stayed there for the next two decades, becoming one of the best chefs of the Frankfurter Hof hotel. It was a double bonanza for my father, who had given up on both his sons at one time.

After my year in Germany was up, I came back to a test set by Mr Kerkar. 'Show me what you have learnt,' he said. And thus began one of the most elaborate presentations of my professional life. I decided to make thirty-two dishes to present to Mr Kerkar.

I had eight notebooks with me, containing all the recipes I had learned in Germany. I chose to make simple dishes starring all the meat groups—chicken, pork and beef, as well as fish and prawns. Each kind of meat featured in four or five preparations. I had ten days to prepare for the presentation, and when I discussed my plan with Mr Mascarenhas, he sounded doubtful.

'Are you mad? How will you prepare so many dishes?'

I persisted. 'Sir, mere ko banane do.' (Please let me do it, sir.)

'Make only as many dishes as you can handle. Not more,' he warned me.

'Please sir, just give me a boy who can help me.'

I enlisted the help of a young kitchen staff member, Bipin, and with some support from Mr Mascarenhas, set to work.

I wrote down the preparation process down to the minutest detail, including all the chopping, cutting, slicing and dicing that needed to be done. I listed all the products required—cream, butter, milk, fresh provisions, dry provisions—and asked Bipin to keep them ready. Two days before my presentation, I started prepping rigorously—marinating the meat, cutting, chopping, etc. It is not necessary to marinate the meat for continental cuisine if you keep it aside for a day. But I did not want to take chances, and determined to get better flavours out of my meat, I went all out by marinating it.

On the day of the presentation, I laid out a buffet of thirty-two dishes in a small banquet room. Mr Kerkar had invited other senior executives to sample the food as well.

I remember walking to Mr Kerkar's office to fetch him. I told him politely that we were headed to the Gateway Banquet Room. He was surprised.

'Why the banquet?'

'Sir, you wanted a presentation, so I put together a buffet for you.'

'A banquet for four dishes?'

I said, 'No sir. I have made thirty-two dishes.'

Mr Kerkar stopped in his tracks. 'What?'

As soon as he stepped into the banquet room, Mr Kerkar looked first at his executives, then the buffet spread and then at Mr Mascarenhas, who simply nodded.

'Yes, he made it himself. With just this one boy to help him out,' he said.

He looked at me. 'How did you put together thirty-two dishes?'

'Sir, you had enough faith in me to send me to Germany. I wanted to show you how grateful I am for the opportunity and give you a glimpse of all that I had learned there.'

'How did you remember all the recipes?'

I showed him my logbooks.

'You were writing there as well?'

'Yes sir. Otherwise I tend to forget.'

Mr Kerkar smiled. He was impressed. And since he could not possibly taste all thirty-two dishes, he chose a few from the spread and sampled them. Here are some of the dishes he tried:

Königsberger Klopse

A German specialty—meatballs in a creamy white sauce with capers. Traditionally, this dish is made with veal, beef or pork, but I made it with lamb and gave it my own twist. The lamb meatballs were poached in a stock of white wine and reduced double cream with stock and then smeared with a mustard-flavoured cream sauce.

Sauerbraten

Sauerbraten is one of Germany's national dishes. It is traditionally made with beef, venison, lamb or mutton, with heavily marinated meat. I went with lamb, which I marinated in red wine, vinegar and herbs. I slowly stewed it in a pan with onion, garlic, beetroot, beetroot juice and little bit of brown sugar. Once the lamb was cooked, the pan was deglazed.

Donner Kebab

Donner kebab is a typical German dish where the chicken is put on a Shawarma machine and then thinly sliced and sautéed well with herbs and a little gravy. It is then put in a roll with lettuce, grated carrot and mayonnaise.

Chicken Schnitzel

A flattened chicken scallop that was marinated in mustard sauce, salt and pepper and then dipped in flour, egg and bread crumbs. The breaded chicken was shallow-fried to a crisp and served with chopped parsley, hard-boiled egg and very finely chopped spring onion.

Fish Orly

Fried fish in beer batter; the batter had a little bit of flour and yeast; beer and seasoning were added and the batter was set aside for some time till it fermented. I used cod fish fingers, marinated with salt, pepper and lemon juice; they were dipped in beer batter and fried to a nice golden brown.

Pork Cassoulet

Pork stewed with vegetables and asparagus

The presentation was successful. And the biggest proof was the letter I received from the personnel department the next day that said I had been promoted. I was to be the new sous-chef de cuisine, second-in-command to the executive chef. It had been only a year and a half for me at the Taj Hotel, and I was already living my dream.

7

Dousing Fire with Fire

With my promotion to the position of sous chef, my relationship with Mr Mascarenhas, which had started off rocky, transformed completely. Over the months, he empowered me to a great extent and started trusting me more and more. Now my interactions with him were longer and more productive.

I began to work on the legendary Taj banquet parties. I was given a free hand to plan the menus for these occasions and thus had to visit the purchase department frequently to order all the raw material that I required for my dishes. One of the senior sous chefs at that time, Mr Jagat Verma, would sometimes have me take charge of service in the evenings whenever he had family commitments. I liked to be left to my own devices, and handling the kitchen on my own gave me the best opportunity to learn.

While Mr Mascarenhas was also around on these occasions, he usually remained busy with his own work and attending back-to-back meetings. Besides, given his seniority, he would not get involved with every little aspect of the kitchen. This was a blessing in disguise for me. If there were problems, I tried to resolve them on my own.

I remember one such incident. A senior director with the Birla group was at Tanjore, the Indian restaurant, with a large group of guests. Unfortunately, we were all struggling to keep pace with the busy service and his order was delayed. He was extremely displeased and complained about the tardy service. I was asked to go meet him.

I took a deep breath. I was determined to win him over and humbly apologised. 'Sir, I am very sorry. We wanted to serve you the freshest food possible, just off the pan. Unfortunately, there were two dishes in your order that had been lying on the counter for a little longer than my liking, and I had to do them all over again.' Was this the truth? Perhaps not. But I had to defuse the tension.

The next day, when Mr Verma asked me if everything went alright, I promptly said, 'Yes sir.'

'How many covers did we do?'

I gave him the number of people we had served, which was high.

'Were there any problems?'

'No sir, nothing in particular. But yes, there was a senior person at a table and he was not happy.'

'Why didn't you call me?'

'I am so sorry, sir. Next time, I will.'

But in my mind, I had been convinced there was no real need to call him—how could I have learned on the job if I didn't know how to tackle these situations myself?

And that's how my stint as sous chef de cuisine continued: making the most of the available opportunities, creating some for myself and always trying to learn on the job.

And then came that fateful day in 1973.

Mr N.B. Daruwala, our food and beverage director, arranged a meeting with all the restaurant managers and Mr Mascarenhas. Mr Daruwala declared he was going to announce promotions. A shiver of excitement ran through all of us. We younger ones were especially thrilled and anxious. He began with Mr Mascarenhas—he was anointed as the new food and beverage consultant. Everyone assumed our sous chef Mr Jagat Verma would be the new executive chef. But the shocker came when his name was announced as the new food and beverage manager. A young coworker, who could barely contain his curiosity, blurted the question, 'If Mr Verma is the new F&B manager who is the new executive chef?'

Mr Daruwala cut him short. 'Why are you so impatient? Anyway, since you want to know who our new executive chef is, he is standing right next to you.'

It took me a few seconds to realise that I was the person he was referring to.

There was a stunned silence in the room.

'Satish?' asked my colleague.

'Yes, Satish.'

I had tears in my eyes. All my hard work, sacrifices and commitment seemed to have borne fruit. I wanted to pinch myself to see if it was even really happening.

I received my promotion letter the next day, and the press went gaga over how I was the youngest executive chef in the world to take charge of a five-star kitchen at merely twenty-six years of age. I was giddy with gratitude and excitement. I was happy and keen to prove myself all over again. And I knew that the real test still lay before me, in the very kitchen which had changed my life completely.

But a commercial kitchen is a tough, unforgiving place. The Taj was no exception. From day one, I knew I would be tried by fire. Even though I had been working at the Taj for five years, I knew people would be uncomfortable taking orders from a twenty-six-year-old. But with every milestone achieved, there is a new challenge to be faced.

The first few days were rocky. Some of the older chefs ganged up against me and began to ridicule and heckle me. Whenever I said something, they would either abuse me in their mother tongues or say something disparaging. Even if you do not know a language, it does not take a genius to understand when you are being abused. They kept mocking me in this way until I approached a dear friend, who knew the language that some of the bullies spoke. I requested him to teach me some strong words in the tongue, in case I wished to retaliate, and I wrote them all down and slipped the paper into my pocket. I never actually used the profanities, but at least I knew what the bullies were saying about me when I wanted to them to follow my instructions. It gave me a pretty fair idea of who would be easy to work with and who needed tough handling. While I was not in the dark anymore, I was not happy about the situation either.

I used to wake up at 5 AM every day, get ready and get to work by 7 AM. My first stop was the Shamiana restaurant, the coffee shop, where I would check on the preparations for the buffet breakfast. Here were several live counters, and I had to check on every little detail—the garnish, the replenishments, the eggs. I also took the opportunity to interact with the guests and find out what they had to say about the food. After that, I went to the room service kitchen that served both the Taj heritage block and the new tower. I was bothered by the fact that despite all the hard work that my chefs and I would put into the food, some time would be lost in delivering it through room service and the food that reached guests would not be as fresh as it could be. I tried to improve on this aspect of room service by reducing the time taken for preparations and ensuring quicker service.

Next, I would settle into my office—those days, there were no computers and emails, and all my memos and messages would be on paper. I would have to go through piles of notes and kitchen logbooks prepared by my chefs on the previous day. They had every little detail about covers served, dishes, compliments and complaints. Besides the Indian restaurant, Tanjore, there was a French one called Rendezvous. Then there was the Harbour Bar and the elite and super-exclusive Sea Lounge, that offered stunning views of the Gateway and the Arabian Sea—a favourite with the swish gentry of the city. Then, of course, there was Shamiana, the coffee shop. We also had a Chinese restaurant called Golden Dragon. Besides these, there were eleven banquet rooms, each of which had a separate logbook. There was also a planning sheet for each of the banquets that was to be hosted on the next day, and I used these books and sheets to put down my remarks, observations and inputs, so that all communication was on record. By the time I would be done with my administrative work, it would usually be time to head to the chef's dining room, where I would share a cup of tea with all my senior chefs who would brief me about their days. And then I would do rounds of the main kitchen, the butchery, the bakery, the hot and cold sections, and the holding area where the finished dishes were kept before service.

I always liked to be hands-on with every aspect of managing the kitchens and the banquets. During lunch service, I would not only make rounds of all the restaurant kitchens to check on the dishes, I would also occasionally interact with the guests to get their feedback. Sometimes, I cooked a few signature dishes for the banquets myself. Around three, I would head back to the chefs' dining room again and along with the senior chefs, taste and dissect one dish from each of the five kitchens every day in order to check on standards and improve upon them. I also conducted training sessions with fresh inductees twice a week, to make sure they maintained Taj standards.

One morning, while getting ready for work, I thought long and hard about my position. My two sous chefs were cooperative, but not as competent as necessary. And I was not able to get any good work out of the others because they were in no mood to cooperate with me. 'You always dreamed of becoming the executive chef,' I told myself. 'Now that Mr Kerkar has given you the opportunity, do you want to give it up without a fight?'

I was on probation for three months, and I knew that if I did not deliver, I would go back to being a sous chef again. There was no saying when I would get another opportunity like this. It was a do-or-die kind of situation for me.

At that time there were quite a few chefs from different parts of the country working in the kitchen. Though I had been working at the Taj kitchen for five years now, when it came to taking orders from me, a twenty-six-year-old, there was plenty of resistance. Perhaps, that is human nature—to be suspicious of anything that is new or unfamiliar. Either way, the chefs did not find it easy to submit to authority when it was wielded by someone who was younger than them.

That day, I walked up to Santan D'souza, the most difficult person in the kitchen. Santan used to be in charge of the fish preparations. Now, as the executive chef, I used to ration raw material in order to control costs. I realised that the chefs were in the habit of hoarding ingredients or asking for more. I also noticed that at one stage, cooks started using lot of oil in the food so I started rationing the oil—in a single day they were using up to two tins of 16 kilos each. I cut it down to one and half tins first and then continued to ration it further. Since Santan handled the fish section, and at times for banquets, he needed to fry a lot of fish, it meant he consumed a lot of oil, which I was rationing. And I could sense he was extremely unhappy about this.

Santan had the habit of leaving a deep-bottomed pan bubbling with oil on the flame. One day, he took the hot pan off the stove and left it on the floor. One of the kitchen trainees accidentally tripped over the pan and was badly scalded. As he began screaming in pain, Santan smacked him on his head and yelled, 'You wasted my oil and this man,' he pointed at me, 'does not give me any oil!'

I was furious but I knew there were others who shared his sentiments and I had to steer them around tactfully.

The next day, I approached his work station and wished him a good morning. He did not reply. I persisted, 'Sir, today on the buffet, we have fillet of pomfret Bonne Femme. I would like us to make it differently this time.' Bonne Femme is a classic French dish made with a creamy sauce of mushrooms and white wine. It was a dish I had been taught by Moncourt, and I knew his version was as authentic as you could ever get in India.

Moncourt had also taught us how to ensure the fish fillet remained super moist and how to extract the maximum flavours from the stock—little tips and tricks that made it one of his most celebrated dishes at the Ashoka.

Santan's style was different. He would arrange the fish in a deep tray, add lemon juice, salt and hot water, and then cover and poach it. He would then remove fish, strain the liquid and make the sauce by adding butter and flour to it. This method made the fish sauce taste floury, but in Moncourt's version, it would come out creamy and glossy.

When I tried to explain the difference to Santan, he snarled at me. 'What? Are you trying to teach me? You are a kid and you dare to lecture me? When they made you our executive chef, we all laughed. You think you know everything, is it?'

I swallowed the insult. 'No sir, that isn't it. I still have a lot to learn from all of you, but since this is how we were taught the recipe at catering college, this is the way you will make it from now on.'

He refused. His body language was not only resistant but defiant. In that moment, something came over me. My prize-fighter alter ego was straining at its leash. I was not the puny boy who had joined the kitchen as a trainee, five years ago. I had bulked up a little. And in any case, as they say, it is not the size of the dog that matters in a fight, but the size of the fight in the dog. I used all my courage to physically push Santan aside and take over his work station. 'I will make the dish and show you how it should be done.'

I enlisted the help of a young chef and managed the station till 3 PM. We kept replenishing the dish for the lunch buffet, and there were no complaints.

Since I was the executive chef, I had to design the menu for the next day. I decided to put Pomfret Caprice on the menu, which is a dish with grilled fish, béarnaise sauce and grilled bananas. The following day, I went in as usual at 7 AM and went to the fish section with the same boy. I started prepping for the dish till Santan sauntered in at 9 AM. I looked at him, and much against my desire and upbringing, I used one of the bad words I had learnt over the last few days. I told him I would throw him out if he did not listen to me again. I kept him away from his station that day till 3 PM, while I made the pomfret dish. Again, there were no complaints from the guests.

On the third day, I put Pomfret Doria on the menu, a preparation that used generous portions of butter. I was in my office trying to finish some paperwork at 7 AM, and fifteen minutes later, I heard a knock. It was Santan. I was still very angry with him and I knew if I lost my nerve at this point, I would never be able to reclaim my position in the kitchen. 'Sir,' he said, 'I am sorry for the way we all have been behaving in the kitchen.' He touched my feet as the traditional mark of respect to a senior. He was much, much older than me and yet he touched my feet! No matter how workplace dynamics worked out, I could never forget my upbringing; the values that my parents had instilled in me. I had to make a point.

I made him sit next to me, put my hand on his shoulder and said, 'Santan, this hotel doesn't belong to either your father or mine. You are a servant here, a chef. I am a servant here and a chef too. What is our aim? To please our guests, make them happy. The company has made me executive chef, so it makes sense for you to do as I say, doesn't it?' He nodded silently and promised to follow my instructions from thereon.

I added, 'If the roles were reversed, you would have made me apologise in front of all your friends. But I will not do that.' I put my arm around his shoulder, and we walked into the kitchen, in full view of every person there. The message was loud and clear. Our employer had put me in-charge and everyone else had to fall in line.

This stand-off in the kitchen made me realise something vital. There were so many people who, despite having slogged it out in the kitchen for years, were nowhere near the position I had been given. Seeing me rise through the ranks so quickly was bound to make them feel bitter, and whatever happened was perhaps their way of testing a young and upcoming chef in their midst. In order to pass these tests, chefs in tough kitchens had to play a tough game. In the boxing ring, you always have a champion and a challenger. That day, I was the challenger who had won an important round in the arena.

8

Stars and My Stripes

As the executive chef of the Taj, I was responsible for the staggering number of parties and events that were hosted in the banquet rooms. Our banquet rooms were popular for their opulent decor, unencumbered views of the harbour and impeccable service and food. It was also a matter of great prestige to host a banquet at the Taj. Some of these banquets were a cakewalk, some challenged my creativity and some were sobering lessons.

I remember a particular dinner hosted by the All India Truckers' Association. This was a unique event. Most truckers and transporters are from the north of the country, with a hearty appetite for simple wholesome food and banter. They are particularly fond of their chicken. Highway fare, as we know it in India, has been served for decades at roadside dhabas, and usually features a dal and tandoori chicken or a chicken cooked in a thick gravy. The distinctive style of food—with generous use of hot spices and butter or ghee, served with chopped onions and green chillies and tandoori roti—is known as dhaba cuisine and has now become a part of restaurant menus as well. But in those days, it was unusual for a luxurious five-star property to replicate these dishes for a banquet.

Since I was born and raised in North India and was familiar with dhaba food, I went in with supreme confidence. I had catered many successful banquets before this and was riding high on my early success. I thought I had it all worked out.

The task was simple—plenty of chicken tandoori to go with the free-flowing alcohol. We were expecting around 300 guests at the dinner and I had planned my portions accordingly. It did not occur to me that a trucker with a robust appetite would consume far more than a five-star regular, who is used to small plates and dainty servings. Besides, instead of 300, twice as many guests landed up. And they were all hungry.

Barely an hour into service, I realised to my utter horror that we were running out of marinated chicken faster than you could say 'kukkad'! I was pretty close to hitting the panic button. I was in a tizzy as I simply scooped up every last piece of chicken available in all the kitchens and began to slather it with whatever marinade was at hand. We had to think on our feet and act fast to save time—tempers were rising in the banquet hall and trust me, no one would like to come in the way of a hungry trucker and his chicken. Instead of putting the chicken pieces in the tandoor, we decided to pan-fry some of them and grill the rest. Besides chicken tandoori, we also served vegetarian and non-vegetarian gravies. It was all hands on board, and after a gruelling three hours of service, we finally managed to feed every last person at the banquet, and all of them left with a happy memory of having eaten at the Taj. Even if what they ate was but a more stylised version of the food they had every day.

During my tenure as executive chef, I was lucky to cater at many VVIP banquet functions. I clearly remember the wedding of billionaire construction tycoon Pallonji Shapoorji Mistry's daughter, Aloo. She was marrying Noel Tata, Mr Ratan Tata's half-brother and the head of several important businesses for the Tata group.

I had already discussed the banquet with Mrs Mistry before she invited me to her home to finalise the menu and other details. Along with Mr P.K. Mohan Kumar, the banquet manager, I went to White House, their residence on Malabar Hill. Mohan and I were sitting on the sofa in their sprawling living room, discussing the menu for the banquet as we waited for Mrs Mistry. Suddenly, I noticed a huge dog advancing towards us. Both of us were petrified of dogs and as it inched closer, we jumped up on the sofa in sheer fear. The dog didn't bark but sniffed around and kept staring at us. Our knees were knocking against one another and our hearts were in our mouths. And just then, Mrs Mistry walked in, startled to see us standing on the sofa. She asked me in surprise, 'Chef, what happened?'

I said, 'Madam, I'm very scared of dogs, especially such big ones.'

'He doesn't bite or even bark!' she tried reassuring us.

I said, 'He may be gentle with you, but he doesn't even know us, and we can't even show our visiting cards to him!'

She smiled, called out to the dog and it went away. It took us a while to return to our element.

Anyway, it took us around two hours to do a broad planning for the menu. Since I had managed several of the Shapoorji-Pallonji family and official events before, I was aware of their food preferences.

The wedding was supposed to see guests from different parts of the world and so I was expected to come up with a menu that would be dominated by continental dishes, with plenty of innovations.

At the party held at the White House, Malabar Hill, with approximately 500 guests in attendance, I had a live barbecue station with Malai Lamb Chops, Creole Prawns, Dill Salmon, Teriyaki Chicken and Saffron Tikka. I innovated with dishes such as the Gunpowder Paneer Tikka (paneer marinated with yogurt and Malgapodi powder and cooked in the tandoor) and Veggie Heaven (a broccoli, mushroom and artichoke shashlik). There was a salad counter, a cold food section, a pasta counter and a hot buffet. We also offered a wide selection of Indian dishes. The desserts were plentiful and took up an entire area of their own.

The show-stealer in this elaborate banquet was the Chicken Strasbourg. This was a breast of chicken stuffed with chicken liver pâté, chopped onions, spinach and garlic mushroom duxelle and herbs. The chicken was then poached till soft and cooked in a creamy sauce with cracked pepper—glossy, colourful and flavourful.

Chicken Saltimbocca was the other most popular dish of the night. It was a scallop of chicken, pan-seared and sautéed with herbs, immersed in red wine with mushrooms and sundried tomatoes. And then there was also a Beckti dish with stuffed black olives in butter, flavoured with lemon juice and a dash of white wine.

A very different incident takes me back to our Tanjore restaurant. Our last order in the evenings was at 11:45 PM as the restaurant would close at 12:30 AM. One night, four guests walked in around 11:40 PM, and we could not refuse them because technically we were still open.

Now, one of the supervisors at the restaurant used to stay in the distant suburb of Borivali and the poor chap was mentally preparing to catch the last train back home when our guests walked in. The supervisor was jittery because he did not want to miss his train. He tried his best to make the guests feel comfortable and tried to sell them something simple and composite—like a chicken curry and rice, chicken tikka or a prawn curry and rice—so that it could be served quickly and easily.

But as they settled down, the table decided to order thalis. A traditional thali is a complex assortment of a variety of items, and before the main thali is served, you also have to serve soup and a beverage like aam panna or chhaas. Our guests were insistent and so I said, 'Okay, we will prepare a thali'.

One of the important elements in a thali is raita, made with yogurt and mint and cucumber. Unfortunately, in our hurry to serve our guests, we completely missed preparing the raita. The guests were fidgety and summoned the supervisor, asking, 'Raita kidhar hai?' (Where is the raita?)

The supervisor, who was preoccupied with getting home, misheard their question as 'Rehta kidhar hai?' (Where do you stay?) He promptly answered, 'Borivali'.

The guests were furious with what they thought was the supervisor's temerity. 'What do you mean? How can you be so cheeky?'

It was a disaster. It took all my persuasive skills and several rounds of 'Please sir, he didn't mean it sir, completely our mistake sir,' to beg for forgiveness and mitigate the issue.

Such incidents were wake-up calls for me. Working in a five-star commercial kitchen, you need to be prepared for all kinds of situations, including your clients' dogs! Planning is key to every executive chef's success. It is as important to understand the number of guests expected or covers to be served, as it is to understand the profile of your guest.

In my years at the Taj in Mumbai, I had the pleasure of catering to famous Bollywood stars, who often had their requirements. Some of them were expectedly fussy, others valued discretion and their privacy. There were a handful who were generous with praise and would happily engage with us. As the executive chef, I was also a brand ambassador for the Taj and I was responsible for handling their concerns carefully. The last thing you would want is for a high-profile patron to walk out.

I had mentioned earlier about my youthful crush on Mumtaz, the actress whose films I would watch several times over. Imagine my excitement when she decided to host her wedding reception at the Taj!

In 1974, Mumtaz, one of the top filmstars of that time, was to get married to businessman Mayur Madhvani, who was settled in Uganda. A lavish banquet for at least 1,000 guests had been organised, and we were expecting almost all of the film industry to turn up, along with the groom's special guests from all over the world.

You can imagine my excitement when Mumtaz arrived at the hotel for a meeting prior to the ceremony. I remember that day vividly. The sales and marketing head called me to meet her in one of the smaller banquet rooms. I was in my crisp uniform, ready with my notepad and pen, a list of items in my head. I walked in, my heart pounding in my head, and Mumtaz was introduced to me. She shook my hand—it was as though a jolt of electricity shot down my spine. The meeting went on for an hour or so, but I was in a daze for the entire day.

Mumtaz was at the peak of her popularity in those days and the wedding was supposed to be one of the biggest star-studded affairs ever. The menu was predominantly Indian, with plenty of Gujarati dishes and some innovations. Mumtaz was particularly fond of butter chicken, and she had told me, 'Whatever else you have on the menu, please include butter chicken.' How could I refuse?

The star of the menu was the butter chicken, along with Boti ka Rogan Josh, Maachi Koliwada and chicken biryani. Some of the vegetarian dishes included a Gujarati preparation called muthia saag and a brinjal dish with raisins and besan, as well as Paneer Makhanwala, Gujarati chips masala, aloo-anjeer kofta in Chettinad sauce. As usual, we had a lavish spread of desserts: I had created a thandai rasmalai and motichoor laddoos with kala jamun in the centre—I called it Kala-Peela because as you would cut through the laddoo which was golden yellow on the outside, you could see the soft black kala jamun centre. Served on a bed of rabri, this dessert won the most appreciation that night for its colourful and unique presentation.

In attendance were celebrity guests such as Dharmendra and Hema Malini, but the party also saw a large number of gate crashers. There was also a massive crowd that had gathered outside the main entrance to the hotel to catch a glimpse of their favourite stars, and at one point, the guests had to be brought in through the back gate of the hotel. Late into the night, the guests had to be escorted out through the kitchen and the back gate to avoid getting mobbed. Such was the hysteria that night!

During the party, however, I got caught in a peculiar situation. Mumtaz had taken up the responsibility of planning the menu with me, since she was familiar with most of her guests and their likes and dislikes. She had also given me strict instructions not to start the buffet service till some of her most special guests had arrived.

The party started, and as expected, the bigger the star, the later they would make an entry. However, Mr Madhvani was getting impatient. His guests were all there and we had not yet started food service. I had the very difficult task of keeping him calm and buying us more time. At 10 PM, I had still not received a nod from Mumtaz, who was nowhere to be found.

The hosts had taken up several banquet and ball rooms for the occasion, and some VIP rooms as well. We had to physically go from room to room to look for her. A little after 10:30 PM, I managed to locate Mumtaz—she was in a VIP room adjacent to the banquet, attending to a 'very special' guest of hers, who was enjoying a drink. Determined not to let anything mar the event, I managed to convince her to start the buffet service because Mr Madhvani was now on the verge of a showdown. Thankfully, she agreed, and what was turning out to be a knife's edge for us, ended up being truly memorable.

Years later, a very different mood prevailed over Bollywood actor Bobby Deol's wedding reception, hosted by his father, the legendary star Dharmendra. Dharam ji was an icon for an entire generation of Indian men, both for his winsome smile and his action hero status. Bobby was his younger son, and he was at his happiest best on that day. I remember the bonhomie that he shared with his guests, and how he wanted a selection of the finest drinks and snacks to be served in the VIP room all through the evening.

Being discreet, nipping potential crises in the bud and enjoying the confidence of your client—these are skills that come to the aid of every executive chef in a high-profile hotel. And I was no exception. Over the years, I had kept the secrets of many of my clientele, including renowned vegetarian industrialists who would come to our restaurants to enjoy a special prawn dish. Or a young Bollywood couple secretly raising a toast to their relationship. We had to take care of them all.

Another incident which I can never forget happened at a dinner I organised for Mrs Indira Gandhi and her family. Though I had catered for her during an international conference, this was a different experience—this time we had to cook for her and her family. One fine day, we got a notice that Prime Minister Mrs Gandhi would be in Bombay with her family, including her sons Sanjay and Rajiv Gandhi, and his wife Sonia Gandhi. We were supposed to cook for the family at the state guest house.

Since they were in Mumbai, I created a very special menu that comprised Maharashtrian and Parsi dishes. The Gandhi family arrived in the evening and I was introduced to them, after which I went on to explain the menu. I elaborated on the origin of the dishes and how they were prepared, and I could feel that the family was quite excited about the offerings. So far, so good. But then Sanjay Gandhi piped up and said that he did not want any of the dishes on the menu, and asked for Chinese instead. I was in a fix. I had not made any provisions for cooking Chinese food at the state guest house, and Chinese food did not taste good unless served right off the wok. In fact, as a chef, I have always been against the idea of taking Chinese food out of the restaurant where it is meant to be served.

But this was Sanjay Gandhi, the second most powerful person in the country. You could perhaps attempt to convince the prime minister to try something different, but I had not heard of anyone who had had the audacity to say no to Sanjay Gandhi, let alone try and make him change his mind!

As soon as I walked out of the dining room, I called my chef at the Golden Dragon kitchen and gave him instructions for whatever I needed—some fried rice, a chicken dish, a prawn dish and some vegetables. I told him that I would come to collect the dishes as there was tight security at the guest house and it would take longer if he sent it. Timing was of paramount importance in Operation Golden Dragon, so I took a police jeep with a flashing beacon and urged the driver to make a dash for the hotel where my chef had the food ready.

I had asked the chef to prepare Golden Fried Prawns, which was a hot dish at the restaurant, Jade Chicken (minced chicken with spinach and Chinese herbs poached and immersed in a flavourful sauce), Konjee Crispy Lamb (shreds of lamb crisply fried in an orange, flavoured sweet-and-spicy sauce), salt and pepper veggies dipped in batter and fried, and crispy honey noodles served with vanilla ice cream.

We dashed back to the state guest house just in time for dinner. I rushed in, quite breathless, to the see that my team had already started serving the Maharashtrian and Parsi food which the family was visibly enjoying. So when I started serving the Chinese food, it was the icing on the cake. As Mr Gandhi dug into the Chinese food with relish, I felt relieved and rather pleased. Later, after dinner, Sanjay Gandhi thanked me for an excellent meal.

Looking back, I think this incident taught me how to always be resourceful in order to avert a possible crisis and how to always prioritise the guests. Had I allowed my nerves to get the better of me, I could not have reached out to Golden Dragon to save the day. The food was fresh and warm thanks to the five-minute green corridor that we got, and we were applauded for the effort.

Helming a bustling high-profile commercial kitchen is never a cakewalk. I was literally baptised by fire. I remember catering for a massive 500-cover banquet for the French Consulate on the occasion of Bastille Day, which falls on 14 July. One of the star items was a baked lobster dish, for which I had to cut the lobster in half, extract the meat and wash it properly to make a stuffing of lobster, prawns, scallops and mushrooms, flavoured with herbs, onion, garlic and celery.

I was supposed to make 300 portions of this dish, and on the day of the event, I sorted the stuffing in a tilting fry pan, which is a big bratt pan. I put butter on the pan and sautéed the stuffing with the other elements, so that it turned a light, golden brown. I was in luck—I was getting the perfect flavour and was extremely satisfied with the way my dish was progressing. I then poured half a bottle of brandy in the bread pan so that I could use half a ladle of this flamed brandy for the stuffing to give it a nice flavour. All this I had done several times before, but somehow, on that day, I seem to have lost focus for a split second.

I slipped and fell facedown into the flaming bread pan. My face felt as though it was on fire! There was a sharp, stinging pain on my eyebrows and my eyelashes were burnt. I could feel the stinging burns on my cheeks as well. I was rushed to the hospital, where I was given first-aid and then discharged after a few injections. I was in terrible pain, but my mind was on the party and the preparations that I was supposed to have completed by then. I spoke to my assistant and he reassured me that the team had finished the dish according to my instructions and that all the guests were now relishing it! That day, I realised the importance of delegating responsibilities, and to have a team that is trained and ready to step in at a moment's notice.

Those were the days when the Taj was the default choice for anyone who wanted to create a special memory for a special occasion. Writers, magazine editors, industry leaders and Bollywood heart-throbs—we had the privilege to serve almost all of the city's stars and cater at all the high-profile banquets and dinners. Social media did not exist and so press coverage could make or break you. Media stalwarts like Vir Sanghvi, Shobhaa De, Busy Bee aka Berham Contractor were extremely fond of me and appreciated my skills. They were true critics who kept me on my toes and brought the best out of me. Write-ups from them brought me tremendous encouragement and recognition.

During my years as the executive chef, I was introduced to some of the leading business tycoons of the day, who would simply pick up the phone and speak to me whenever they wanted a customised menu for a grand party or something special for a more intimate, private dinner. This included Dhirubhai Ambani, Aditya Birla, M.K. Sanghi, Ismael Padamsee and Yogender Mafatlal. During my Taj journey, I made some great friends and saw future stars take shape before my eyes.

The Taj was synonymous with Mumbai, the city of dreams. The city that nurtured the finest culinary talents to impress the new breed of foodies that the country was now home to.

9

A Chutney Surprise

My strong foundation in European cooking techniques came in handy when I began to experiment with Indian dishes. I could marry the best of both worlds and experiment with new dishes that would excite and surprise my guests as well as myself.

One of the dishes I tried very early on at the Taj, was a spicy and colourful spaghetti. All I did was mix a little bit of green chilli, turmeric powder, paprika powder, chopped spring onions, chopped onions, garlic and coriander leaves with tomato sauce. The result was a colourful flavour-bomb. When I presented this dish to my chefs, they liked it since it was pungent and offered a familiar yet exotic kind of spiciness. We decided to name it Spaghetti Burmese. While serving it to guests, the team garnished it with a whole green chilli for a dramatic effect.

Of all the things that I tried in the kitchen, I enjoyed the process of reimagining a home-style recipe the most. Give me a traditional dish and I would put it back on the table with a nice little tasty twist. For instance, I developed a home-style chicken curry, for which I used some chicken tikka from the tandoor, sautéed it with onion, garlic and chopped spinach and presented the dish as Chicken Tikka Palakwala. The idea behind every dish is always to pique your curiosity.

Then there was the restaurant favourite—a rich beef bolognese. I wanted to give it a different spin altogether, so I replaced the beef with minced lamb and made a sandwich out of it with grated cheese. It packed all the creamy deliciousness of a bolognese into the convenience of a sandwich and voilà! It was a surefire hit!

Whenever I carried out my kitchen experiments, I would first serve the dishes to the executives of the hotel gathered for lunch. I would take their feedback and then tweak, improvise and improve my dishes. The kitchens were my laboratories and I saw myself as an alchemist—mixing, matching, blending, pairing, unpairing and stirring it all up into something new, unexpected and always fun.

Once my experiments began to be well received, it added fuel to the fire of my imagination. But I also worked with a handicap—most of the chefs I worked with belonged to the old school of thought, preferring to fall back on traditional wisdom, recipes that had been handed down by word of mouth, and a hesitancy to push the boundaries. I had to lean on whatever books and magazines I could get to expand my knowledge.

My dishes were my stories. I had my own language. I used my learning, my reading and my understanding of the grammar of cooking to create my signature style, with some quirky touches for effect. A slit green chilli where you least expect it, a fistful of tropical fruits in a savoury dish, completely new marinades for traditional dishes—I tried it all.

When you are in a Taj kitchen and you are open to experimenting, there is no end to the kind of dishes you can conjure up. I found inspiration in everything around me. I saw jars of sweet mango pickle that came from Gujarat and

I wanted to pair the pickle with a creamy white sauce for a new chicken dish. I used a marinade of garlic, red chilli paste, a little lemon juice, salt and pepper, and then I breaded the bird. I chopped up the mango pieces from the pickle, added some extra cream to the white sauce and mixed in the chicken. It turned out to be a bloody good dish! People loved it, and I was happy with my creation.

Post my training in Germany, I was a different person. Earlier, I had mostly followed my instincts and drawn from my training at the catering college to create standard dishes. Now I realised I had more knowledge about ingredients and techniques and more clarity about the finer points of cooking. My training in Germany, combined with my time in the Taj kitchen, gave me the confidence that I was capable of handling all the cooking ranges—roast, grill, oven—on my own. But the commercial kitchen is not a place for solo players. Even if your ideas are your own, you need a team of well-equipped, supportive and experienced players to turn that dreamy dish into reality. I can never forget those helped me on this journey—Chef Mascarenhas, Chef Verma, Chef John, Chef Cosma, Chef Shetty, Chef Anand, Chef Camillio, Chef Bento, Chef Louis. I consider them to be my real gurus.

The main kitchen was divided into different sections, and even before I became the executive chef, I was attached to the continental roast section and the soup sections, and had free access to the Indian or tandoor kitchen. I used to spend a lot of time in these kitchens and departments, interacting with the chefs, talking to them and gathering inputs for my experiments. Later, when I became executive chef, I continued with my experiments. I made quite a few standout, strong dishes that were put on the Shamiana menu, when the restaurant launched in 1973.

I experimented with the traditional chicken tikka. I put the chicken tikka pieces on skewers and put them in the tandoor. In some cases, I even experimented with other kinds of marinade for the tikka. I used soy sauce, barbecue sauce or pesto sauce, or even coated the pieces with yogurt and put them in the tandoor. The result was always something of a surprise—tangy, sweet, pungent. I wanted to see if one can move beyond red chicken tikkas and bring in different flavours, colours. At that time, five-star coffee shops did not go beyond the usual mayonnaise-and-cheese sandwiches—perhaps a colonial legacy. But we were catering to a different and young India, and I wanted to give them something more interesting. I took the bold decision of introducing a spicy burger—using meat from a Rogan Josh—and it simply took off. It was later introduced at the more formal Sea Lounge as well, and remained there on the menu for years.

In 1973, Shamiana, the all-day dining experience with an Indian and international à-la-carte menu, was launched to replace the existing coffee shop. As the executive chef, I was responsible for the launch. We had a lavish buffet for breakfast, which at that time, no other hotel was offering. From day one, we saw long queues of youngsters at Shamiana for the Shamiana club sandwich, prawn cocktail, masala burger, Goa prawn curry and chicken dhansak.

Perhaps one of my most popular innovations at the Shamiana was the chicken tikka sandwich, which again was born from the idea of adding something different and fun to the regular coffee shop menu in a five-star hotel. I wanted to create a dish that would appeal to everyone, from an older person and a globe-trotting gourmand, to a young, fun-loving person on a night out. Earlier, I had tried the chicken tikka sandwich as an experiment for the room service menu and received some honest feedback from the guests that had helped me improve the dish. When it was finally introduced at Shamiana, it changed the concept of five-star coffee shop menus for good.

These dishes were perfect to have with a cold beer or a light drink, and the coffee shop began to attract a younger crowd that was excited by the new additions to the menu. I even put a spin on the Parsi classic dhansak and served it with bread, and people just loved it. I used to see them sopping up the gravy with the bread—it is quite satisfying to see people relish your food in this way.

The Mongolian Barbecue theme in the open-air section of Shamiana after sunset was also a hit with tourists. This is where we would serve unlimited salads and the tenderest meat—that would be wok-tossed and grilled. There was always a waiting list for the Barbecue on weekends and we held it for over six months, back when Bombay had cooler weather till the monsoons.

There was plenty of scope to innovate for the banquets too. Once, for an important party, I made a lobster dish and named it Lobster Kika after my daughter Kanika! In the Indian kitchen, I made a bhindi dish, to which I added grated cottage cheese. I named it Punneri Bhindi after my son Puneet.

This reminds me of a kofta I made for a party hosted by Mr Aditya Birla. I named it Desi Twist. It was a paneer and raw banana kofta with raisins, walnuts and mushroom sauce. The kofta had butter-sautéed onions, garlic, ginger, thyme, parsley, paprika powder, dhania powder and jeera powder, mixed with boiled and mashed raw banana and paneer. I coated the koftas with semolina and fried them, and added them to a continental-style sauce flavoured with a puree of mushrooms.

In my opinion, what you name your dish is very important. Even if you are cooking with the most familiar ingredients, you can excite your guests and give them a new experience simply by presenting and naming your dish differently.

I also developed a dish known as Gosht Keema Ghotala, which was minced lamb cooked with Indian spices and freshly ground herbs and spices. When the keema was on the verge of being done, I took an egg slurry, put it into the keema and scrambled it. I served the dish at the Taj Residency coffee shop in Bangalore, and I am told it did very well.

On another occasion, I created a special pulao rice with butter chicken for a banquet Mr J.R.D. Tata was hosting for Zambian President Kenneth Kaunda. First, I made a nice, velvety butter chicken with small dices of chicken. I then created a pulao out of it, which was more like a biryani, and I named it Butter Chicken Pulao.

I also created a dish known as Shahenshahi Kofta. It was created for Mr Amitabh Bachchan just around the time his film *Shahenshah* had released. I remember I was vacationing in London at that time, staying at St James' Court with my family. Mr Bachchan, I heard, was also at the same hotel, shooting for a film called *Jhoom Barabar Jhoom*; as was his son, Abhishek. In fact, Abhishek was on the same floor as us and we would exchange pleasantries whenever we met. And it was during one such quick conversation that I asked him if his father was happy with the food being served at the hotel. Mr Bachchan was a regular at St James and the staff knew of his preferences, and the family was being well looked after, he said. Even then, I let him know that I had created a kofta dish specifically for him and would be glad to serve it to him.

A couple of days later, the intercom buzzed in my room and Abhishek told me that his father wanted to taste the Shahenshahi Kofta I had mentioned. I quickly went into the kitchen—St James being a Taj property, I was familiar with the kitchen. The Shahenshahi Kofta was prepared and served alongside the khichdi that he had ordered:

Shahenshahi Kofta for Amitabh Bachchan

A kofta made with potatoes, mixed veggies, chopped mushroom and paneer, spiced and mixed with coriander, jeera, red chilli powder and bit of chat masala. I added diced anjeer and pista and stuffed the kofta with it. The kofta was rolled in sooji and crisp fried.

I made a sauce which was a combination of a makhani sauce and chicken tikka masala sauce. But I took care to make a thin sauce, not a very rich or spicy one, tempered with mustard seeds and curry leaves, and had it served to him in his room.

I also remember the dish I prepared for former American President Bill Clinton. My first interaction with him was on an aircraft when I was handling the Taj flight kitchen—I was one of the privileged few allowed on the charter he was using to travel to Bhuj from New Delhi. I distinctly remember he was wearing a black shirt with jeans and blue suede shoes. He was larger than life and yet a very friendly person, who acknowledged and greeted everyone around him. I was introduced to him by a member of the American Consulate. I was pleasantly surprised with his knowledge of Indian food—he knew about butter chicken, biryani, naan and surprisingly enough, there was even a mention of raan (lamb leg). He asked me which part of India I was from as I served him his meal, which he thoroughly enjoyed.

The following evening, I met with him again at the Taj property in Ahmedabad (he was no longer the serving POTUS and was there to take stock of the condition of those affected by the devastating earthquake in Bhuj). I was surprised when he addressed me by my name, 'Chef Arora, so nice to see you again!' I had prepared a special dish for him. For the dish, I had taken a large brinjal and slit it open, without cutting it completely. I made a minced lamb with some spices and cheddar cheese to use as stuffing. I then immersed the dish in a marinade of yogurt, rolled it up in silver foil and put it in the oven for about five minutes. Then I put it on a bed of charcoal and also covered it with charcoal and put it back in the oven for about twenty-five minutes. When I took it out, it carried a beautiful flavour. Mr Clinton was very, very happy, saying that he had never tasted such an original and tasty brinjal dish!

The other dish I created for Mr Clinton was raan. I first boiled young lamb with masala until it became absolutely tender. I then immersed it in thick pomegranate juice and then seared it with onion, garlic and tandoori masala. I then put the dish in the oven. It became so delicious and so soft that I was surprised to find Mr Bill Clinton eating with his hands. It was a completely satisfying experience.

I also experimented with desserts. There is a pudding I created for Prince Charles for a banquet he was throwing for Asian industrialists at Warwick Castle. I named it the Bombay Pudding, and it was a combination of sponge cake, gulab jamun, rabri and rasmalai. First, we put in a bit of the thin rabri at the base of the glass in which we were to serve the pudding. Then we decorated the glass with chocolate leaves, after which we added the sponge cake and gulab jamun mixture to the rabri, topped with a little rasmalai, and then covered it again with sponge cake and a bit of chocolate sauce. We finished the dish by adding custard on top.

I also did a Portobello mushroom dish—I took large Portobello mushrooms, washed them, blanched them quickly and put them aside. I then made a stuffing of shiitake mushrooms, button mushrooms and wild mushrooms with onions and herbs and Indian masala, and used it for the Portobello mushrooms. I slathered the mushrooms with korma sauce, sprinkled generous amounts of cheese on top, and baked it. Those who tasted it said it reminded them of the Thermidor sauce, and I was inspired to put this dish on my kebab festival menu. It received great feedback from food bloggers, the media and guests.

I have always enjoyed mixing the same ingredients in different ways to get new and delicious results. This is how I have kept my creative juices flowing and my guests satisfied.

10

Around the World in Many Plates

The Taj kitchen was so much more than just a physical space, and my work took me to every part of the world, places where I had the opportunity to cook, learn and create new culinary stories, while showcasing the best of what India has to offer. Ms Camellia Panjabi, our marketing director, and Mr Kerkar suggested that I visit Hong Kong, China, Pakistan, USA, Germany and Thailand, to learn their cuisines and help launch specialised Taj restaurants in India. I saw myself as my country's culinary ambassador and of course, a representative of Taj's legendary hospitality.

I have very fond memories of visiting Hong Kong, where I was asked to try out and learn more about some of the best hotels and stand-alone restaurants in the 'New York of the East'. I returned with a deeper understanding of Szechuan cuisine and introduced it at our Chinese restaurant at the Taj, the Golden Dragon. The restaurant opened its doors to the public in 1973, which went on to open the floodgates to the wild, wild popularity of 'Indian Chinese' cuisine, that continues to hold sway over our people today.

Until Golden Dragon introduced Szechuan cuisine, India was familiar with the Cantonese and Hakka Chinese that was popularised by Chinese immigrants in Kolkata's two Chinese settlements, way back in the 1920s. As the cuisines began to travel to other metros, they began to acquire an Indianness, as chefs started using Indian spices and condiments, especially by adding ginger, garlic and the ubiquitous green chilli to these traditional dishes.

Such was the popularity of the food we served at Golden Dragon that it spawned an entire street food culture that mimicked the dishes at the Taj at a fraction of the price and authenticity.

Golden Dragon was a labour of love and tremendous planning. We put together a team of chefs for the launch that included Chef Michael, Chef Brando and Chef Baby, who were from popular stand-alone restaurants across Hong Kong. Our first manager was Frankie Lock. We sourced the best ingredients from our suppliers in Hong Kong and put together a menu that was authentic and would appeal to Indian tastebuds. We didn't cut any corners and Golden Dragon eventually became one of our most successful properties in India and overseas.

I have the fondest memories of Gulzar, the Peshawari restaurant at Taj President, which was launched in 1982. For this project, Mr Kerkar sent me to Pakistan to do research on the local cuisine. This was probably the best research trip I ever went on; I was joined by Mr Subir Bhowmick, one of the general managers, and Chef Arvind Saraswat.

Even in those days, it was very difficult to obtain a visa for Pakistan. But our employers ensured we got it, and we started our research in Lahore, followed by Islamabad and Peshawar. All through our stay, we were under heavy security cover. But that did not interfere with the gastronomic journey that we had embarked upon. We ate our way through our stay—whether it was food served at the roadside dhabas or in the kitchens of the ustads or from masters of kadhai cuisine originated in Peshawar.

Kadhai cuisine is characterised by the use of cast iron kadhais and absolutely no water for the cooking of meat. The technique gives the meat a smoky, robust flavour as you scrape off the dry spices from the sides of the kadhai as you cook. The meat cooks in its own juices. In its birthplace, kadhai cooking had a different dimension to it altogether.

Every restaurant or stall was attached to a local butchery and displayed rows upon rows of fresh lamb. They sold the dishes by weight. So when you placed an order for say 1 kilo of kadhai lamb, they would slice the lamb in front of you and cook it on a very high flame with freshly ground spices, converting it into a mouth-watering dish served in the kadhai itself. Every kadhai preparation was meant to be shared and eaten with freshly baked naan to polish off the last traces of the meat and masala. There is something special about the act of sharing a kadhai full of freshly made food, using your fingers to eat and licking them clean. The whole experience was a celebration of the emotional bond that we share over food in our countries that have so much in common. The memories of our Peshawar adventure still make my mouth water.

From 1985 onwards, I was made the culinary director for the western and southern regions of the Taj Group of Hotels, and became involved with Taj Coromandel and Taj Connemara Chennai, Taj Fisherman's Cove, Taj Malabar Hotel in Cochin, Taj Westend and Taj Residency in Bangalore, Taj Lake Palace Hotel Udaipur and Taj Banjara in Hyderabad. The executive chefs of these elite properties all reported to me. I worked closely with them to create menus, new restaurant concepts and design kitchens across these properties.

I was also instrumental in opening the Admiral Plaza Hotel and the Princeton Hotel in Dubai for the Taj Group and travelled extensively within the USA, especially California, to work with celebrity Chef Wolfgang Puck and study the local cuisine.

It was sometime in 1982 when Ms Camellia Panjabi called me to her office and said that she and Mr Kerkar wanted me and two of our dynamic managers to go to Los Angeles and study what was being celebrated as Californian cuisine at Chef Puck's high-profile restaurant. I was thrilled. Wolfgang Puck was one of the most talked-about chefs in the world who catered to Hollywood A-listers and Oscar parties.

Californian cuisine is not as distinctive or as unique as, say, Italian. But it was Puck who put it in the spotlight by mixing the freshest and finest ingredients with flair. He made farm-to-table a fashionable concept as he advocated the use of locally produced, ethically sourced ingredients in plated dishes with a lot of French influences. This was the essence of the Californian cuisine that Puck was popularising.

When I met him, Puck was thirty-three years old and his restaurant Spago was very popular as a fine-dining destination among the well-heeled of LA. It was always packed. The kitchen always buzzing. It was quite an experience watching Puck in action—taking rounds of his kitchen and the restaurant, shouting his orders and plating his dishes, exuding an undeniable charisma.

Among the most popular of his signature dishes at Spago at the time was the pizza with smoked pink salmon and caviar. It was a thin-crust pizza with a finely herbed tomato base, loaded with smoked salmon and caviar and grated parmesan. The other dish that was popular with the patrons was the Chicken pot pie—diced chicken marinated with oregano and thyme for a while, and with a dash of white wine for another half hour. The wine was then removed and the chicken dredged with flour and sautéed and cooked in a creamy chicken stock and made into a pie with broccoli and mushroom, topped with cheese. There was also his Weiner Schnitzel—chicken escalope with bread crumbs and shallow-fried with hard-boiled seaweed, and served with caper sauce.

One of Puck's most famous dishes—something that he served at an Oscar party—was the Fish Puff Pastry. Essentially, it was a puff pastry shaped like a fish (something he cut out on a cardboard), with layers of puff pastry and fish that was baked to perfection with caper sauce.

Puck was also very fond of making threads of veggies—he had a machine that would cut carrots or cabbage in the shape of noodles, which he used liberally in many of his dishes. One of my favourites from his repertoire was a salmon with pesto sauce, in which he used sauteed vegetable noodles with lemon-flavoured olive oil and olive butter. And there was also a starter—baked potato stuffed with caviar. He boiled a large potato, halved it, scooped it out to make a frothy creamy mashed potato, stuffed it back with caviar and cheese on top, and baked it. It was divine!

These are just some of his dishes that fascinated me, and later I tried to use his ideas and elements in some of my dishes at Rendezvous (what later became Zodiac Grill) and other VIP and black-tie galas.

During the days that I spent at Spago, learning from Puck through close observation, there were some things that he said that impacted me deeply. He believed, 'The most important element of any dish are the ingredients. They are the base.'

Many times, he told me, 'Chef Arora, if you have a restaurant that's serving good food, do not only depend on good food. A restaurant becomes popular only when supported by its service ... Being a great chef is not enough, you have to be a great businessman.'

But over and above everything else, I remember his cooking philosophy: 'Cooking is like painting or writing a song. Just as you use colours and notes to make a creation, you need flavours to make a good dish. You only become good when you how how to mix all these flavours and get the best from your ingredients.'

Later, I helped Taj Group launch a Californian cuisine restaurant at the Admiral Plaza, where I tried to imbibe some of my learnings from my days with Puck.

Thai Pavilion at Taj President in the serene neighbourhood of Cuffe Parade, South Mumbai, was another concept I spent a lot of time developing. In 1990, I went to Bangkok along with Ajoy Mishra, GM of Taj President, to research the cuisine, eat Thai food and pick up the essential ingredients. We spent days in an agricultural institute in Bangkok and brought back with us seeds of makroot, galangal, kaffir lime and lemongrass, which we then planted in the farms of the Taj Group in the suburbs of the city. We figured India, especially Mumbai, and Bangkok had similar climates and the herbs and spices could be cultivated easily here.

We selected two female chefs from Bangkok to head the project. They could barely speak English but were unbeatable in the way they executed Thai cuisine. Thai Pavilion eventually opened its doors in 1993 to fabulous reviews, with Anand Solomon as the executive chef.

The Taj literally took me places. In the early 1980s, I was invited by the press club of Switzerland to conduct one of the first Indian food promotions in the country. This helped us add to the bottom line—when guests read about these festivals usually held over three to four days, usually Thursday, Fridays, Saturday and Sunday, there was high footfall in a short time. We did seafood nights, Hyderabadi festival, dhaba festival—which was also known as Arora Da Dhaba—Far East Asian festival, kebab and biryani festival. We usually held these festivals by the pool side, because I believe in live cooking, which is best done in an open area.

I would set up temporary kitchens and more than half the cooking was done live. You would find lobster being barbecued and oyster being gratinated in front of the guests, Koliwada Surmai being fried in a kadhai, Goa prawn curry heating in earthen pots on a sigree, pomfret fish with chutney wrapped in banana leaf being cooked on lava stone. There would also be a display of raw sea food on crushed ice. The visual, aural and aromatic drama would not only whet the appetites of our guests, but also leave them drooling.

For the dhaba festival, we recreated a dhaba by the pool side with charcoal sigris and the food displayed in huge vessels. Guests were seated on charpoys. There was a sugar-cane-juicing cart, lassi being churned with a wooden beater that had a ghungroo attached to it, and rotis were being made in front of the guests in traditional tandoors. Gurda Kapura Kaleji was prepared on a tawa. This food festival was great for our business.

The Hyderabadi food festival also was a great success with haleem, biryani and patthar kebab. Marinated meat was cooked on stone that had also been marinated in oil, saffron, garlic etc., imparting more flavour to the meat. These gimmicks—if you may call them that—helped us in creating successful food festivals in India before we began to replicate something similar in hotels abroad.

This was followed by the Culinary Olympics organised by and at Hotel Okura in Osaka, Japan, where I won the prestigious Escoffier Chefs' Gold Medal. Chefs from Italy, Spain, United States and France had participated in this event. I was accompanied by Chef Anil Ashokan. Each chef was given a restaurant to showcase their cuisine. First, a host of journalists and a panel of judges tried the food that the chefs had prepared, then the restaurants were opened to the general public, whose feedback on the food was also taken into consideration for the final evaluation.

I played to my strengths and turned the spotlight on tandoori cuisine and regional Indian food, which was not known or had not been explored in Japan before then. My team and I put up a staggering display of Indian herbs and

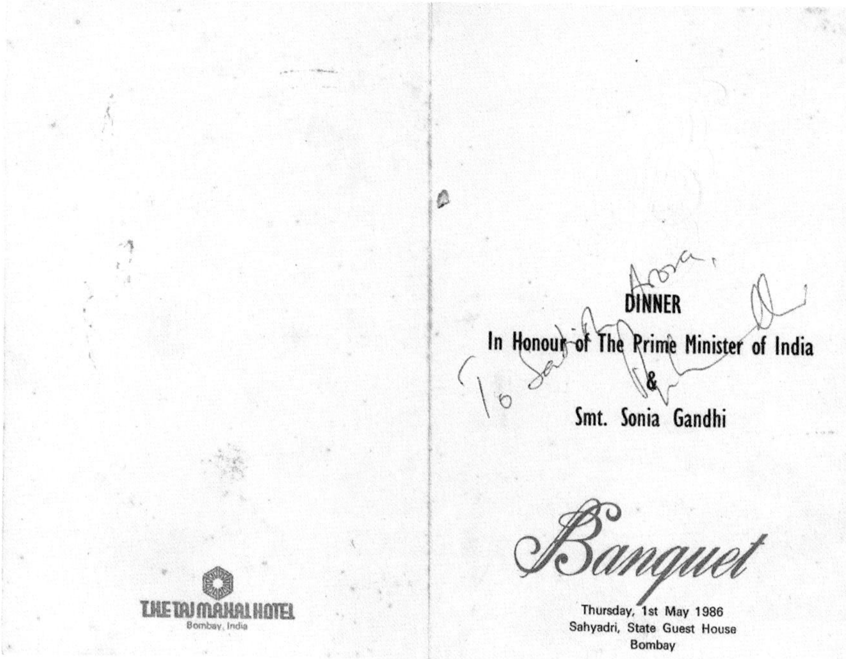

THE TAJ MAHAL HOTEL
Bombay, India

DINNER
In Honour of The Prime Minister of India
&
Smt. Sonia Gandhi

Banquet

Thursday, 1st May 1986
Sahyadri, State Guest House
Bombay

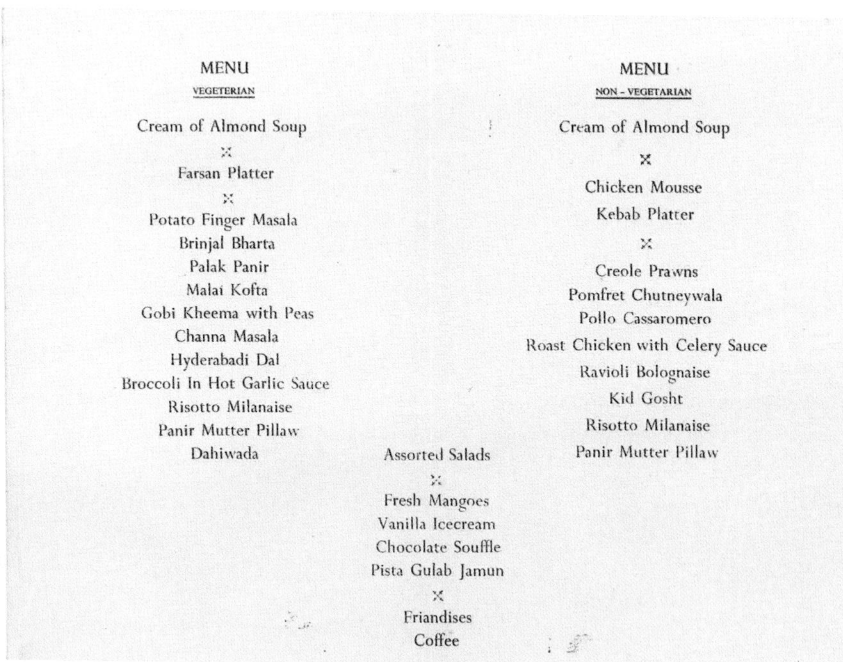

MENU
VEGETERIAN

Cream of Almond Soup

Farsan Platter

Potato Finger Masala
Brinjal Bharta
Palak Panir
Malai Kofta
Gobi Kheema with Peas
Channa Masala
Hyderabadi Dal
Broccoli In Hot Garlic Sauce
Risotto Milanaise
Panir Mutter Pillaw
Dahiwada

MENU
NON - VEGETARIAN

Cream of Almond Soup

Chicken Mousse
Kebab Platter

Creole Prawns
Pomfret Chutneywala
Pollo Cassaromero
Roast Chicken with Celery Sauce
Ravioli Bolognaise
Kid Gosht
Risotto Milanaise
Panir Mutter Pillaw

Assorted Salads

Fresh Mangoes
Vanilla Icecream
Chocolate Souffle
Pista Gulab Jamun

Friandises
Coffee

Menu for a dinner hosted in honour of Prime Minister Rajiv Gandhi and Mrs Sonia Gandhi by the chief minister of Maharashtra Shankarrao Chavan at the state guest house in Mumbai on 1 May 1986.

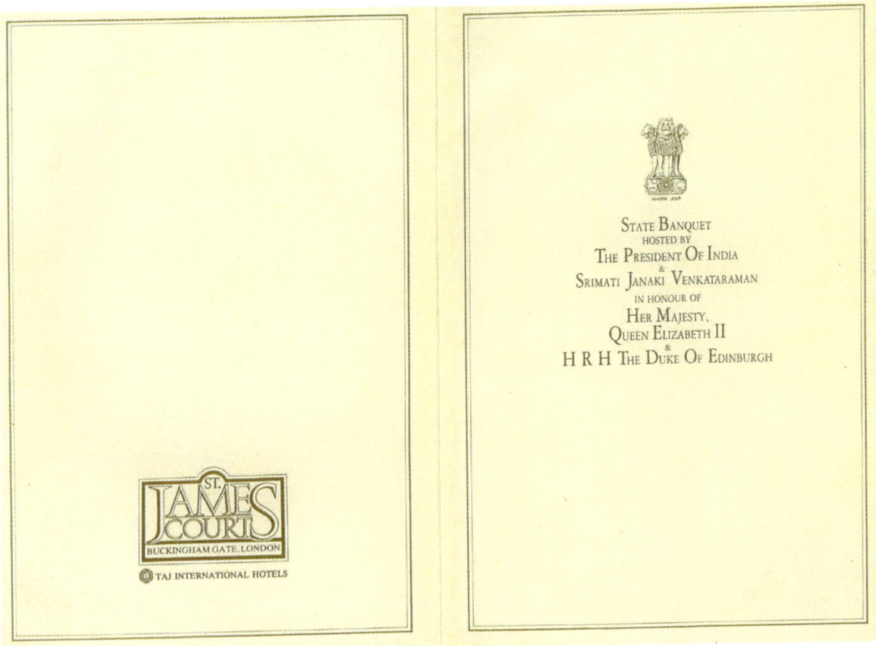

Menu for a state banquet hosted in honour of Her Majesty Queen Elizabeth II and HRH the Duke of Edinburgh by President R. Venkataraman and Mrs Janaki Venkataraman at St James' Court, London, on 5 April 1990.

सामिष

धनिये की सॉस में विशेष सब्जियों का मिश्रण

* * * * *

झींगा व चावल के चीले का व्यंजन

* * * * *

संतरा, नींबू व पोदीने का ठंडा शर्बत

* * * * *

भरवां मुर्ग बादाम सॉस के साथ

पके आलू व गुच्छी

पालक का सूफ्ले

* * * * *

आम व रसभरी का मिष्ठान

* * * * *

कॉफी

AMUSE BOUCHE

LES TROIS PARFAITS DE LEGUMES EXOTIQUES
AUX COULIS DE CORIANDRE
Delicate combination of three exotic vegetables
perfumed with fresh coriander sauce

*****

CREPES DE RIZ FARCIES ET HOMARD A L'AMERICAINE
Rice pancakes with lightly herbed lobsters
and a moussline of American sauce

*****

SORBETS MAISON
Orange, lemon, melon and mint sorbets

*****

POUSSIN GRILLE "NOTRE FAÇON"
Poussin stuffed with saffron rice, minced lamb,
peppers, grilled and served with lightly spiced almond sauce

GRATIN DE POMMES AUX MORILLES
Sliced potatoes baked with morels

SOUFFLE D'EPINARDS
Spinach souffle

*****

ASSIETTE DE MANGUE ET CHARLOTTE DE FRAMBOISES
A very light mousse of mango and fresh raspberries

*****

CAFE—PETIT FOUR

राष्ट्रपति भवन, नई दिल्ली.
भारतमें ब्रिटिश हाई कमिशनर,
सर डेविड गुडॉल द्वारा वॉटर कलर

५ अप्रैल १९९०

5th April, 1990

Rashtrapati Bhavan, New Delhi.
Water-colour by Sir David Goodall,
British High Commissioner to India.

निरामिष

धनिये की सॉस में विशेष सब्जियों का मिश्रण

* * * * *

खुम्भ से भरे चावल के चीले

* * * * *

संतरा, नींबू व पोदीने का ठंडा शर्बत

* * * * *

सब्जी व ऐस्पैरगस् के साथ हल्के तले बैंगन

* * * * *

आम व रसभरी का मिष्ठान

* * * * *

कॉफी

AMUSE BOUCHE

LES TROIS PARFAITS DE LEGUMES EXOTIQUES
AUX COULIS DE CORIANDRE
Delicate combination of three exotic vegetables
perfumed with fresh coriander sauce

*****

CREPES DE RIZ FARCIES AUX CHAMPIGNONS DES BOIS
Rice pancakes stuffed with wild mushrooms

*****

SORBETS MAISON
Orange, lemon, melon and mint sorbets

*****

LASAGNE D'AUBERGINES ET BEURRE BLANC
Sliced aubergines, pan-sauteed,
layered with asparagus and vegetables,
and laced with butter sauce

*****

ASSIETTE DE MANGUE ET CHARLOTTE DE FRAMBOISES
A very light mousse of mango and fresh raspberries

*****

CAFE—PETIT FOUR

राष्ट्रपति भवन, नई दिल्ली.
भारतमें ब्रिटिश हाई कमिशनर,
सर डेविड गुडॉल द्वारा वॉटर कलर

५ अप्रैल १९९०

5th April, 1990

Rashtrapati Bhavan, New Delhi.
Water-colour by Sir David Goodall,
British High Commissioner to India.

प्रधान मंत्री

Prime Minister

New Delhi
October 8, 2000

Dear Shri Beri,

I would like to thank you for organising the excellent Indian cuisine for me during my recent visit to the United States of America. The culinary skills of the chefs Shri Arora and Shri Oberoi . contributed significantly to making the trip an enjoyable one.

I wish you all success in your professional career. Please also convey my best wishes to the chefs.

With regards,

Yours sincerely,

A.B. Vajpayee

(A.B. Vajpayee)

Shri D.K. Beri
Director (Business & Corporate Affairs)
Taj Palace Hotel
2, Sardar Patel Marg
Diplomatic Enclave
New Delhi.

A note of appreciation from Prime Minister Atal Bihari Vajpayee for the meals catered for him during the Millennium Summit at the United Nations, New York, in September 2000.

Taj Air Caterers

Sector -- **DEL - BHUJ** - **Hi-Tea**

ASSORTED FRESH JUICE

Orange Juice, Anar Juice, Coconut Water,
Creamy Cold Coffee

REFRESHMENT CANAPES

NON-VEG	VEG
Smoked Salmon Pate	Cheese Mousse
Cheese Mousse	Asparagus

HOT SNACKS

Shammi Kebab	Masala Aloo Cashew Samosa
Do Nali Kebab	Cholia Kebab
Chicken Curry Patla	Paneer Ka Soola
Vermicelli Prawn	Pickled veg cheese Barquet

CLOSED S/W

Chicken Montedella	Paneer Bujee S/W
Tandoori Raan S/W	Dosa Aloo S/W

CHAT

Palak Pakoda, Papri Chat

DESSERT

Pista Kesar Rasmalai
Caramel Toffee Mousee

Assorted fresh fruits from Baskets

Tea / Coffee

Menu for a meal served to former US president Bill Clinton on board a chartered flight during his visit to Bhuj, Gujarat, after the earthquake in 2001.

4th April, 01

Dinner Order from

His Excellency William J. Clinton

At

Room No. 318

Ambi Pana

--x---

Shikandri Raan
Kakori Kebab
Tandoori Aloo
Malai Murg Tikka
Chicken Tikka
Lal Raan (Seekh Kebab)
Tandoori Pomfret
Paneer Tikka
Tandoori Plain Naan

-----x ------

Palak Paneer Pasanda
Dal Ummed (Dal Makhani)
Bhuna Gosht
Chicken Biryani
Assorted Indian Bread
Mix Vegetable Raitha

----x-----

Desserts

Shahi Tukra
Gajrela
Gulab Jamun

Tata Filter Coffee from Coorg

Menu for a meal served to former US president Bill Clinton at the Taj Gateway, Ahmedabad.

Satish Arora at a food festival at the Southern Sun Elangeni & Maharani Hotel, Durban, South Africa, 1993.

Satish Arora on completing twenty years with the Taj Group of Hotels, displaying his medals.

spices, with a detailed presentation of the blend of spices in our culinary traditions, which served as an eye-opener for the guests. Before each service, I made it a point to talk about Indian cuisine and its heritage, and this went down very well with the guests. I even had a dedicated English-to-Japanese translator for this purpose.

I received extensive coverage in the Japanese media, which was quite impressed with the serpentine queues outside our restaurant. It did not stop there. The Taj Group sent me back to Japan after a few years to oversee the development of their Dehydrated Indian Gravies products, which were then sold at SOBU supermarkets across the country.

Ms Panjabi and Mr Kerkar also wanted me to get involved with Bombay Brasserie in London, and Raga in New York. Since I was executive chef of the flagship hotel in Bombay, they involved me in the process of developing the menu and training of the staff. Bombay Brasserie was the most talked-about Indian restaurant in London in the 1980s, as it had shown the courage to break away from tradition and serve dishes like sev puri in a fine-dining ambience. Bombay Brasserie continues to serve traditional Indian flavours to a discerning clientele.

All through my professional life, I have developed many dishes, but nothing gives me more satisfaction than a dish that is well received. It is a satisfying and humbling feeling when people associate me with a dish completely and recall it fondly as 'a dish by Satish Arora'!

11

The Perfect Papaya for Mrs Gandhi

During my decades as the executive chef at the Taj, I had the privilege to cook for some of the world's most powerful men and women: presidents, prime ministers, Hollywood stars and industrialists who were nation builders in our times.

When Dhirubhai Ambani's elder son Mukesh, now one of the richest persons in the world, got married at Cooperage, I was in charge of the banquet that catered to hundreds of guests. It was a traditional affair with a lavish vegetarian spread, and I was responsible for creating imaginative and delicious vegetarian dishes that would appeal to his eclectic guest list.

I created a fusion cannelloni with a creamy cottage cheese filling and tender bits of pineapple to add to the dish's delicate flavour. I made a stuffing of onion, garlic, celery, chopped spinach, grated cottage cheese, black pepper, herbs and a white sauce. I stuffed it into cannelloni rolls, put it in a serving dish, coated it with cream sauce and herbed tomato sauce and baked it with cheese. Mr Ambani's younger son Anil was responsible for the banquet and he was so pleased with this particular dish that he suggested I call it Cannelloni Arora. The same dish was later served at other high-profile banquets as well. It was part of the classic Taj menu for two decades, alongside twenty-six other signature dishes that I created over time.

Some of the most challenging assignments for me as executive chef were creating dishes for heads of states. When the former President of France Francois Mitterrand visited India, the Taj staff was told that he was extremely particular about his food and was bringing his own chef for the trip. The consulate also sent us a list of ingredients in advance so that my team and I could source everything for this trusted cook. But I was keen to please the French, and the only window available to me was the first evening that he landed.

Now, I was familiar with the French consul of the time, thanks to the many banquets we had hosted for them. So at a dinner where he was present, I decided to talk to him about the president's schedule and how we could possibly get an opportunity to cook for him. 'Sir, I believe you have written to our general manager that he is bringing his own chef. You are familiar with my cooking. Is it possible that we get a chance to do something for His Excellency at least once during his two-day trip? Why don't we do a little food trial in a few days—a three-course meal for you, after which you can take a call?' I pitched.

The consul general agreed and I set about putting together a very French three-course meal.

For the first course, I made a smoked salmon cigar filled with pâté. For the second course, I made a corn-fed chicken breast, with a stuffing of onion, garlic, herbs, mushrooms, cream cheese, spinach and nutmeg. I stuffed the chicken, wrapped it in silver foil and baked it in the oven to cook in its own juices. Once it was cooked, I poured the juices into a pan, added some white wine and cream, and reduced the mixture to make a sauce to pour over the chicken, which I served with fresh vegetables. The aroma was divine. For dessert, I went Indian, but in a Baked Alaska way. In a ramekin, I mixed sponge cake with pistachios, crushed praline, kulfi and gulab jamun, and covered the whole thing with meringue. I then baked the mixture. It was then flambéed with brandy and served.

The French consul seemed impressed with all three courses and promised me that he would speak to the president upon his arrival. On the day of his arrival, around 3 PM, the French Consulate called me and said that the president had agreed to have dinner in his room. We were expected to serve him and the first lady, as well as the consul general and his wife.

I immediately sprung into action and set up a temporary kitchen adjacent to the suite that the president was occupying. I had two assistants with me and we started preparing the food.

I stuck to the menu I had created in collaboration with the consul general. At that time, smoked salmon and pâté de foie gras were considered to be the finest delicacies. After that meal, the accompanying French chef spent the next two days of his trip in the swimming pool—on Mitterrand's request.

I am also thankful to God for giving me the chance to be in close contact with Mr J.R.D. Tata, our chairman and the godfather of Air India. The Tata group company's headquarters are situated in Bombay House, and we had to supply lunch for all the directors of Tata Sons daily. We would send over the food every day, which would be heated up in the pantry and served to the directors in the dining room.

Mr Tata was a genuine gourmand. He particularly appreciated an elegant grilled fish, while his palate for Indian food was confined to a Goan-style prawn curry or a Parsi-style patrani machhi (steamed fish in coriander paste, wrapped in edible leaves) or dhan dar patio (a celebratory rice, dal and fish preparation). But he did not like his food to be spicy. Since I was the executive chef, it was my responsibility to put together the weekly menu and send it for Mr Tata's approval. I looked forward to his inputs on the menu every week: 'See to it that this is not too spicy, or this is not too buttery.' As always, I maintained a logbook with these inputs.

One day, Mr Tata asked me to meet him in person to discuss the menu, since he had some time on his hands. It was 3:30 PM in the afternoon and he was sitting in an easy chair in his office. I pulled up a chair next to him and began reading out the menu to him. He sat with his eyes closed, speaking up only once in a while.

'That roast chicken, will it be skin on?'

'No sir, it won't have skin,' I said.

'Will it be big pieces or small pieces?'

'Sir, it will be a piece of the thigh as chicken breast becomes tough. Sir, I am going to deglaze it with white wine and I am going to use mushrooms and onions and herbs. But I just want to make it clear that since we do not have fresh herbs at the moment, I am going to use dried herbs.'

'Okay, don't put too many dried herbs in that case.'

His feedback gave me tremendous confidence. It is not every day that the chairman of the world's most respected group of companies interacts with you in this way. Working together with my team and catering for the Bombay House lunches was a fun and fulfilling experience that I looked forward to every week.

Mr Tata also entertained at the Taj a lot. He always hosted important formal banquets, lunches and dinners for state dignitaries and other VIPs. He was an early eater, so whenever I was told that Mr Tata was on his way, I would personally take care of his food. Since I knew what he liked by then, I would take the liberty of customising a few things for him. If, for instance, there was no fish on the menu, I would still make a fish dish. Always 'with compliments from the chef'.

Mr Tata's other favourites was a Jade Chicken, Chinese-style, which was a minced chicken with spinach, poached and then immersed in sauce. He also enjoyed grilled prawns, a simple chicken curry or Parsi dhansak, or a nicely roasted chicken with light brown gravy.

One of the biggest challenges and opportunities that came my way, courtesy Mr Tata, was catering for the Commonwealth Heads of Government Meeting (CHOGM), held in Goa, hosted by Prime Minister Indira Gandhi in November 1983.

I had a very tough interaction with Mrs Gandhi—she just met us for a minute or so, but her team had briefed us on how the banquet was a matter of the country's prestige.

The same was also conveyed to us by Mr Tata, who came to the Taj to meet all of us and said, 'The food and service has to be top-class'.

It was an extremely high-profile retreat with leaders from more than forty countries, and their teams, coming down for a mere forty-eight hours. Mrs Gandhi wanted new heritage cottages to be built on the Taj Goa property by the deadline, and the entire Taj Group machinery was in full swing. There was a section on a hill in Fort Aguada, where six new cottages were constructed for Mrs Gandhi, Her Excellency Mrs Margaret Thatcher and all the other state premiers.

Goa, in those days, was not as well-developed. It was a tremendous task to get any work done. Mr Kerkar was our managing director and vice chairman at that time, and he took complete charge of the project. He dealt with the contractor, the labourers, even picking up a broomstick here and a spade there, to expedite the process.

I was busy upgrading the kitchen and trying to make it as hygienic as possible. I put up a huge board in the kitchen where I wrote down the name of the country, the dietary preferences of the head of the state and any other vital information. The guests arrived a day before the conference and were supposed to dine at the restaurants. It meant we had to make sure all the restaurants on the property were ready from the get-go.

The trick to catering to such a large and diverse group of guests is to create a grand buffet. And that's what I did. I put together a vast buffet with more than a hundred dishes for breakfast, lunch and dinner, keeping in mind the setting, the mood and the weather. For the conference, I created a menu of dainty finger foods with visual appeal. I prepared small potato vadas and gobi pakodas, chicken tikka, puffed pastry pies and open sandwiches. I also had to keep in mind everyone's personal preferences—someone did not like coriander, someone did not touch garlic or chillies. But you cannot make twenty different kinds of potato vadas and you also cannot stick to traditional recipes for the sake of it. So I tempered the vadas with curry leaves, mustard seeds, cumin seeds and created an assortment of dips to go with them.

After the conference, the guests were more relaxed—swimming or playing tennis or enjoying the breeze and the views. The mood was jovial and everyone was in flowery T-shirts provided by the Taj, or in their beach dresses and shorts. To make sure everyone had a good time, we were working extra hard to ensure the food was perfect. We had to ensure there was enough fresh fruit, fresh juice, freshly baked croissants and rolls. I had provisioned for an Indian breakfast with upma, poha, dosa that would be made live at the counters. We prepared unique stuffings for mini dosas, including paneer bhurji, soya keema, spinach mixed with cottage cheese and minced lamb masala. And of course, potato for anyone who liked to keep it authentic.

As I have said earlier, I love the concept of live cooking, and it is something I pioneered in India with the many food festivals and barbecues that the Taj hosted. The aroma of food being cooked live not only gets people hungry, but the food is also fresher and tastier. What makes it better is when the chef himself interacts with the guests, explaining a bit about the ingredients and techniques. The more your guests engage with the food being served, the more value it adds to the dining experience.

So for the main banquet, we went all out. There were jalebis and gulab jamuns that were being fried and dunked in sweet syrup, fresh lobsters were being grilled, oysters in colanders, and an assortment of sauces poured on a big roast joint. We also had Shehenshahi biryani in a handi, kept on a lightly burning charcoal sigree, a pasta station with morel sauce, Indian kebabs from a charcoal pit and even Indian breads that were being freshly prepared in a portable tandoor. At every counter, each guest was given plenty of choice—whether it was the cut of meat, the fruits or the sauces. The idea was to make people feel that everything was being customised according to their individual palates. They were floored!

There were at least fifteen hygiene inspectors and doctors that had come along with the various heads of state. It was a nightmare. They went through the cold storages, they checked every inch of the kitchen, the storage area for the raw material—whether vegetarian and non-vegetarian ingredients, fish and lamb were stored separately. To appease them, I even went a step further and made date tags for every ingredient. Containers with cooked food are tagged so that we know at a glance when exactly it was cooked and by when it should be consumed. It helps us in the hospitality industry to ensure a first-in, first-out cycle of cooking and consuming. Date tagging is particularly crucial in flight kitchens.

Some kitchens also have coloured date tags for each day of the week, so that the kitchen staff can tell at a glance when that tray was prepared and by when it should be consumed. The same system is used in the butchery for the meat rack—fresh meat is tagged with the date of arrival, supplier's name, weight, etc. This helps in keeping food contamination at bay and reduces wastage.

But for all my careful tagging, there was invariably a slip-up. At 3 PM, one day, I took a round of the walk-in cooler where the trays were tagged and kept. Everything was in order. Forty-five minutes later, a hygiene officer from Singapore, who was accompanying their prime minister, wanted to take a tour of the kitchen and the walk-in cooler with me. The moment we walked into the cooler, we spotted a handi full of white sauce on the floor instead of on pallet.

The officer was furious about how we were unable to take care of what was a very basic requirement. I tried to salvage the situation by showing him the chart that recorded my last check, how we had tagged every single item and apologised profusely for the oversight. My assistant chef Prem Kumar also joined me and the two of us did our best to convince him that the incident was truly an aberration. Fortunately for me, the rest of the kitchen was absolutely spic and span and assuaged the inspectors' concerns. But those were some of the toughest days and nights for me.

The lavish buffet spreads would turn out to be easier to pull off than the challenge posed by the humble papaya.

You see, the CHOGM retreat was supposed to put Goa on the world tourism map. The retreat saw a flurry of activity—roads were widened, jetties and bridges built, street lights revamped and the airport overhauled.

While the world was only aware of the abundance of the exotic and fine ingredients that were being procured to appease our discerning guests, we were fighting a different battle in the kitchen. A very uniquely Indian, very local and a rather peculiar one, at that.

According to the brief we had received, Mrs Gandhi wanted papaya for breakfast every day. And so did some other guests. The CHOGM was being held in November. Where on earth would we get so many naturally ripened papayas in Goa at that time of the year? Do remember, this was in the early days of tourism in Goa and what one takes for granted these days—ready availability of local and international produce—was not as easy to come by then.

Anticipating a lack of consistently good papayas in November, I had arranged for raw papayas to be brought in from Bombay and had wrapped them in paper to hasten the ripening process. I never do things half-heartedly. Even if I am serving something as simple as papayas, I will leave my stamp on the dish. I'd cut the fruit in a different way, sculpt it, or use cocktail sticks and some mint leaves to make it look pretty.

As it happened, on the very first day of service, the person in-charge of the papayas had left a couple of pieces a little too long in the paper, and they had turned squishy. During breakfast service, we were down to these last pieces of papaya when we were told that Mrs Gandhi and her special guests were about to step in. We were in complete panic. There was no way I would serve overly ripe, soggy papaya to our prime minister, and that too without any presentation value. I was in tears!

I consulted the general manager of the property at that time, Asha Rishi. A police jeep was arranged for me to be whisked off to the nearest market to look for ripe papayas. I got lucky and picked up a dozen pieces of the fruit.

I felt like a warlord travelling in a police jeep, being escorted by men in uniform, whizzing past the villagers with my twelve papayas in tow. The moment I reached the hotel, the hotel security and members of the special protection group stopped me. They had been given strict instructions not to let anyone or anything in without checking. And no amount of explaining, begging and pleading would help us get the papayas past them. Finally, they agreed to let the papayas through after making holes in each of them to check for explosives. I was disappointed, but we used our skills to manage anyhow, and the final result was rewarding, and of course, relieving.

After the service, Mrs Gandhi walked up to us and said she wanted to speak to Mr Tata. We were nervous and worried sick. Mr Kerkar saw us walking behind her as she approached the telephone. He was dead sure something had gone terribly wrong. She said, 'J, this is Indira. I am very proud, J. Your boys have made this country proud.'

When it was time for the guests to leave, they flew back directly from the temporary helipad that had been set up on the property. I remember Mrs Gandhi taking the time to speak to everyone. I was present in my chef whites, as was my outstanding team. Praises were pouring in for all of us. The Australian premier, the Japanese prime minister and other leaders congratulated Mrs Gandhi for the retreat and the arrangements, and thanked us as well. I plucked up the courage to ask Mrs Thatcher, 'Madam, I hope everything was okay. I hope you liked everything.'

She said, 'Remove your cap, chef.'

At that time, we used to wear cloth caps, not the disposable ones that you see today. Mrs Thatcher took my cap and signed it. At that moment, my heart pumped up to a hundred times its size. I looked at everyone who was there—all the senior government officials, the Taj team—and then I looked at Mrs Gandhi. She put her hand on my shoulder and said, 'Well done, my boy!'

At our next meeting, Mr Tata shook my hand and said, 'You have done the country proud, the hotel proud.'

After Goa, I got another opportunity to cook for Margaret Thatcher in India in 1987. I decided to prepare a Goan-style prawn curry. She appreciated it so much that she recommended my name for an event due to be held in London a few months later. The then president of India, R. Venkataraman, was hosting a banquet for the royal family and the who's who of the British Parliament, at St James' Court. I was flown in and was even given an etiquette lesson in how to greet the Queen, were I to meet her. In India, we are used to vigorously shaking hands when introduced to someone, but here, I was told to lightly hold two of her fingers, bow down and call her Your Majesty—no 'ma'am' or anything like that. At the end of the meal, the Queen of England and the Duke of Edinburgh approached us and I was introduced to them. I was not expecting either of them to say anything, but to my utter delight and disbelief, she stopped, looked at me, and exclaimed loud and clear, 'Well done, chef! That butter chicken was just superb.' The Duke of Edinburgh, meanwhile, asked me if I was from South India, because his favourite dish had been the dosa stuffed with wild mushrooms and lobsters. The same butter chicken was eventually served at a Dubai restaurant I was associated with briefly. As was the Goan prawn curry that Mrs Thatcher enjoyed.

These memories make me emotional. If you ask me, these words of appreciation, these rewards are my lifetime achievement awards. I don't really care about promotions or positions as much as these priceless experiences that no one can ever take away from me.

12

A Very Hands-On Prime Minister

When I got into this profession, all I wanted to do was to cook good food and serve it with love. Never in my wildest dreams could I have imagined that someday I would be cooking for the most famous men and women in the world. That the hands that had once tried to make a kheer in a humble family kitchen and failed, would one day rustle up special meals for charismatic global leaders and venerated presidents and prime ministers from across the world. My tenure with the Taj Group of Hotels gave me not one, but several such opportunities. Serving your country's prime minister is a matter of pride and honour, and I would happily say, one of the biggest achievements of my five-decade-long career.

Besides catering for Mrs Indira Gandhi, I also had the privilege of travelling with Shri Atal Bihari Vajpayee when he was prime minister of India. I had the honour of interacting with another prime minister of India, Shri Narasimha Rao, when he travelled to London and stayed at the St James Hotel, a Taj property, and I was responsible for fulfilling all his food and beverage requirements. I also met and interacted with Shri Rajiv Gandhi in Bombay, though he was not the prime minister at that time.

I will always remember my interaction with Vajpayee ji with the deepest reverence. He was a very simple man, who knew how to appreciate even the smallest things. I was thrilled, when in 2000, I was told by our then Managing Director Mr Krishna Kumar that I had to travel with Prime Minister Atal Bihari Vajpayee to New York, where he was to attend a meeting of the United Nations. My first task was to find out about the prime minister's food likes and dislikes. The prime minister's office helped us out with the details and also provided us with his schedule. I planned a menu down to the last detail.

A colleague and I accompanied the prime minister on the Air India flight, along with a media contingent, a few of his closest ministers and Mr Naresh Chandra, who was the ambassador to the USA at that time. Taj–Singapore Airline Terminal Services (Taj SATS) air catering was in-charge of the food, and I was responsible for Taj SATS. Special food had been prepared for the prime minister, while the others were served casseroles.

Before service commenced, I was introduced to our honourable prime minister and I can never forget his smile—so warm, so genuine, more precious than any grandly worded compliment. In New York, Shri Vajpayee was put up at the famous Waldorf Astoria, where we had been given a room as well. We were told that the prime minister was expecting a steady stream of visitors and dignitaries for the three days and nights that we were staying there, and we had to be ready with refreshments and meals at all times. The focus, however, was on tea and accompaniments.

We hit the ground running. The first thing we did was hold a meeting with the executive chef of Waldorf Astoria, and requested him to help us source the ingredients required for the menu I had planned for the prime minister. We needed a variety of fresh and exotic vegetables—broccoli, zucchini, asparagus—and fresh spices like mint, rosemary, basil. I had brought along the dry spices from India. We had been allotted a special area in the kitchen and a couple of chefs to help us with the preparations.

I rolled up my sleeves and got to work. The aroma of the spices filled the kitchen. I had made coriander powder, cumin powder, fennel powder and garam masala. Wherever I go, the first thing I do is roast my masalas and grind them. It is my signature move in the kitchen; the opening act of my culinary theatre. I strongly believe that Indian cuisine is what it is because of freshly ground spices. You can never achieve the same result with mass-produced packaged spices. The aroma of Indian spices has a certain magic that can mesmerise even the most cut-and-dried person in the kitchen. Here too it worked beautifully. As I went about dry roasting and grinding my masalas, the American chefs were drawn to my corner, intrigued by what was happening.

They were full of questions and I offered for them to watch me and ask me questions, while tasting and trying out the masalas. The kitchen was buzzing with excitement and bursting with aromas. On one end, chefs were cooking lobsters in white sauce and on the other, we were creating an Indian garden of spices.

For breakfast, the next day, we had planned to make upma, poha, shira, dosa and uttapam. We had been given a griddle for the dosas. I got down to work, rubbing a slice of onion on the griddle, sprinkling water, brooming it, rubbing the onion again and sprinkling some more water. The American chefs simply couldn't believe their eyes. I had to explain to them that to prevent the dosa or uttapam mix from sticking to the base of the griddle, it was important to season the tawa and prepare it beforehand. They had not seen a dosa being prepared before, and loved how it tasted. And for those used to the latest non-stick cookware, this would definitely seem like an alien concept.

Some of the other dishes I prepared were masala grilled fish, achari aloo, dhingri matar, chicken saagwala, Kerala fish curry and different types of dal. I also made kheer and malpua for our prime minister because, even while entertaining dignitaries from all over the world, we wanted to retain a real and authentic taste of India. In order to bring in some variety, I made mozzarella and soya masala dosa, and cheese and broccoli uttapam.

I created some snacks like Malabari paratha wraps stuffed with arbi-mushroom masala, cheese-chilli avocado toast, chicken and palak pakoda, chakri aloo—which is paneer stuffed tandoori aloo—dhokla pizza, cheese-baked khandvi, Bombay bread pakoda stuffed with masala aloo and mini croissants with chicken tikka masala.

I also made different flavours of chicken tikka, like kesar, chutney, Thai marination, peri-peri and malai. I served the chicken tikka with coconut mayonnaise chutney. As a sweet snack, I prepared a suji halwa gulab jamun tart.

As I had been appointed as the prime minister's personal chef when he was travelling, I had the honour of catering to him on several occasions. One such trip was to the Taj Kumarakom Resort and Spa. Vajpayee ji had taken this trip in order to relax after his knee treatment. One day, during his trip to the lake resort in 2001, I had organised a chaat party in the lawn in front of the cottage where he was staying. I made gol gappe and dahi batata puri, samosa chaat with chana, aloo, imli ki chutney, the works.

I began to prepare the gol gappas for Vajpayee ji when he stopped me. 'It is more fun when one does it himself,' he said and began to crack open the puris with his thumb, and fill them with masala and chutney. I was stunned and remember telling myself how lucky I was to be able to serve a prime minister who was so grounded, so rooted, that he did not hesitate to throw protocol out of the window and use his hands to enjoy something I had made for him.

Eventually, he spotted the samosa chaat and asked me what it was. Once I explained the dish to him, he was like a child, asking me questions about how best to savour it. He readily went with my suggestion of breaking down the samosa into small chunks to let the chutneys cover every morsel, and dug into a plate of spicy samosa chaat with great relish. 'Arre wah!' he kept saying between mouthfuls. What an experience it was!

The next day, he went on a boat trip around the Vembanad Lake, and I was seated next to him. There were no photographers on the boat, but I asked one of the staff to click my photo so that I could keep it as a memento. I would always remember him as someone who spoke less, but observed everything. Whenever I served him food, he would ask me very precise questions about the ingredients and the cooking technique. His was curious and creative.

Let me share another beautiful memory from Kumarakom. I was preparing aloo tikkis for the prime minister and his family in the open area of the resort, when he saw me and said very quietly, 'If you fry this on a tawa, it will be crispier'. I immediately proceeded to fry the tikkis on a tawa, prepared a special chutney to go with them, and when I saw him use his fingers to enjoy the perfectly browned and crisp tikkis, dipping them generously in the chutney, I felt overwhelmed with gratitude—could anyone ever get such an opportunity?

When we were in Kumarakom, Vajpayee ji had asked me about the local cuisine and the use of coconut milk. I prepared some dishes from Kerala with coconut milk in moderation—just the way he liked it. After this, he had attended the South Asian Association for Regional Cooperation (SAARC) summit in Colombo, which I have fabulous memories of accompanying him to. I was responsible for preparing the food for seven other dignitaries from different countries as well. I remember creating a special lobster curry which was well-appreciated by former Pakistan President General Pervez Musharraf.

After the summit, Prime Minister Vajpayee had a brief interaction with the press on the flight. He spoke about his meeting and also thanked me and my colleagues for dishing out authentic and flavourful food.

Of all the heads of states I have had the honour of serving, I would certainly rate my days as Shri Vajpayee ji's personal chef as among the most inspiring. It was a great learning to be so close to such a wise, sensitive and humble person, and I was lucky to have spent a considerable amount of time with him, travelling with him to various destinations.

In my career of over fifty years, I can remember every meal I served to our former prime minister. I have the memory of an elephant, you can say. But more than the facts of what I cooked, what has stayed with me over all these years is how much value every meal added to my life.

When he passed away in 2018, I watched the state funeral on television and was transported to the days when I cooked for him. I remembered his warm smile, his quiet dignity, his down-to-earth nature and his love for the finer things in life—soulful food, poetry, nature and fulfilling conversations. It took very little to impress him, but he gave back much, much more in his appreciation.

13

Taking Flight from the Taj Kitchen

When you spend as many decades as I have at the Taj, you are expected to play different roles at different points in time, often even being called upon to resolve challenges. One such challenge was the flight kitchen.

Sometime between 1996–97, Mr Kerkar requested that I spend some time at the Taj flight kitchen, as it was not in good shape and there had been a spate of complaints about the food. So I started dropping by a few times every week. A couple of years later, in 1999, our MD Mr Krishna Kumar called me to his office and said that they would like to officially 'loan' me for a year to Taj Air Caterers. 'We still need some more improvements and we want to better the business,' he said. And so began my journey at the Taj flight kitchen.

At that time, Taj was catering to twenty-three airlines. The major ones were Singapore Airlines, Delta, Air France, Jet Airways, Air India, Cathay Pacific and Virgin Atlantic. Given the sheer number of airlines we serviced, we had to put together at least two meal presentations or samplings for a new menu for each airline. This happened every year, before the airlines introduced new menus.

It is difficult to imagine the buzz, the frenetic pace of activity, the precision that went into running a large flight kitchen for those who are now used to dehydrated poha and instant noodles, even on overseas flights. A great deal of planning and careful execution went into preparing each tray of food, with attention to the tiniest detail and respect for the cultural sensitivity of the many airlines that had to be serviced from one kitchen.

Controlling temperature, ensuring freshness of the ingredients with relatively short shelf life, ensuring every meal looked, tasted and 'felt' the same, all portions were exactly the same, managing the pantry so that at no stage does one fall short of the best ingredients; packaging and labelling and storing according to the flight schedules—it is a hive out there, with the staff working round the clock, like a machine.

At the time I started working at the Taj flight kitchen, we had to stick to their instructions for each and every dish that the airline listed in their menus. My first presentation was for Singapore Airlines. As per the norm, they sent us their menu, but I wanted to do more. I wanted to show them the skills we had mastered in our kitchens and went out on a limb by adding a few of our dishes to their menu.

When the team arrived for the tasting, I gave them a quick tour of the spread that I had put together.

I had found that the menu would have a few very common Indian dishes such as a kofta and a Rogan Josh. I wanted to do things differently—like a zaika gosht or a chutney gosht. They were quite impressed, and even though we had also created dishes as per their recommendations, they replaced at least 60 per cent of their menu with our suggestions.

I was told this was the first time that Singapore Airlines had done something like it. I was happy with this small but significant milestone.

And that is how, what was supposed to be an arrangement for one year, continued for nine years and my work at the airline kept on challenging me in the most creative ways.

The first such creative challenge happened a few months after I had joined in 1999. Singapore Airlines created a culinary panel by inducting world-class chefs for different cuisines. They wanted someone from the Taj team to also be a part of the panel, and that's how I joined a group of celebrity chefs, including George Blanc from France, Gordon Ramsay from the UK, Yoshihiro Murata from Japan, Alfred Portale and Nancy Oakes from the USA, Yeung Koon Yat from Hong Kong and Dietmar Sawyere from Australia. Chefs like Gordon Ramsay, George Blanc and Nancy Oake are celebrities in their own right, who own their own restaurants. Blanc even owns vineyards. I was the only chef there who was working for a company.

To be on the Singapore Airlines panel was a matter of prestige. We had been told that the airline wanted to be the best in the world in terms of service and food, and impressing them was our job. For long-distance international flights, food is the one thing that passengers trapped in the aircraft look forward to. When you are done watching movies, playing games and sleeping, food is what keeps you entertained and cheers you up.

The chefs had to design and develop menus for first class, business and economy. I was to come up with sixty Indian dishes for Singapore Airlines every year, and present these dishes twice a year in Singapore to the big bosses of the airlines. The dishes were tasted, discussed and the menus were finalised after a great deal of thought. The airline liked what we had created so much that it began to print our names on the menu cards handed out to passengers, with a caption saying: 'Specially Created by Culinary Expert Satish Arora from India.' It was a moment of pride for both me and the Taj.

So how did I go about it? I did not want to create totally new, unfamiliar dishes and confuse passengers who wanted a simple Indian meal. I wouldn't be onboard to explain to passengers what each dish meant or how it was cooked. So I decided to use my tried and tested strategy of giving familiar dishes an unfamiliar and perhaps exotic twist. I thought of the kofta, which is a familiar Indian dish. Most people would have tried one or several variations of it at some point or the other. So I created a kofta with grated cheese, potatoes and crushed dry fruits.

I began to push myself with every presentation. If they expected thirty dishes, I gave them forty to choose from. It was perhaps a shade easier for my peers from the USA or Australia. If they were cooking a supremo of chicken, they would only have to make one main element, accompanied with sautéed vegetables. But in my case, if I prepared a lamb curry, I had to plan for rice and an accompanying vegetable dish, because Indian food is considered incomplete without these elements.

I would try out these dishes in our kitchen, put together all the elements of the meal and take photographs to create an album for my satisfaction and visual reference. I would send the list of ingredients to the Singapore kitchen well in advance, where I had also enlisted the help of a native to source the ingredients. I put in a lot of effort in the pre-production and the presentation of the food, demarcating the dishes with coloured ribbons according to the class—first, business or economy. Even for first class, when we were expected to plate the food in foil packs, I was not happy and instead used plates so the crew would learn how to serve the food correctly. It was an enriching experience for the crew and an important step towards standardisation.

I enjoyed the whole presentation process. After all, I had built my career on the foundation of my pitching and presentation skills. I loved to explain how each dish had been planned and put together, why I had used certain ingredients, and how they should be plated and served to the passengers. I would take pride in explaining how when you serve white rice with yellow chicken, you should also serve a spoonful of green spinach because people eat with their eyes as well. And on a long flight, our eyes are always looking for something pleasant and enticing.

There are so many factors that we have to consider while planning an in-flight menu. While as a hotel chef, you can serve a light and airy soufflé, you cannot do the same in an airline. You cannot serve food which is very strongly flavoured or too spicy, food which cannot be kept for more than twenty-four hours or withstand temperature variation. The Indian fare for the Indian sector was mostly North Indian dishes such as a vegetable kofta or Rogan Josh. I started introducing dishes from various regions of the country. Since the airlines operated around thirteen flights from different Indian cities, this worked.

Eventually, I introduced a varied menu that featured traditional and innovative dishes that I had created over the years.

We offered Dhokla Chaat, Idli Salad, Nimboo Jhinga, Pudina Mirch ke Scallops, Bhopali Seekh, Rangeeli Mirch ka Jhinga and Murgh Chaat as starters. The main dishes featured Kozhi Varutha Kuzhambu, Andhra Pulao, Baingan

Kalwa Gujrati, Prawns Moily, Kadle Gassi, Haleem, Chooza Pista Zaffrani, Alucha Kofta Tamatri, Dhaba Gosht, Khumb Paneer Rogani, Murg Alishan, Chana Dal Gosht and Akhrot ki Roongi. The desserts were also revamped to include Kala Peela, Bombay Pudding, Corn Carrot Kheer and Thandai Phirni.

In 2002, Taj entered into a partnership and collaboration with the Singapore Airline Terminal Services (SATS), then a subsidiary of Singapore Airlines. Subsequently, Singapore Airlines and SATS parted ways, though the Taj continued its association with the catering company. At that time, SATS was the largest airline catering unit in Singapore and had two units, one to cater exclusively to Singapore Airlines, serving 50,000 meals a day at SATS1 and 30,000 meals per day at SATS2. They also had a separate unit that catered to other international airlines. This partnership was extremely fruitful as it helped us get new ideas and acquire technical expertise.

Taj SATS proved to be a fruitful partnership. It was set up such that the chairman was from the Taj Group, while the MD or the chief executive officer (CEO) of the company was from SATS. We had a regular staff exchange programme. The SATS staff had more experience since they prepared far more meals than us at Taj, who churned out only 25,000 meals from our flight kitchen.

The SATS kitchen was a giant factory with teams managing sections dedicated to each airline, working as per their schedule to ensure the food was ready on time. So in order to get more experience and knowhow of the industry and recent innovations and trends, we used to send our chefs to SATS for two weeks for training and when they came back, they brought with them knowledge and expertise. The SATS partnership also helped us gain access to chefs who specialised in different cuisines such as Japanese, Italian and French.

Meanwhile, ever since we had convinced Singapore Airlines to go with our original dishes, more and more airlines had started doing the same. The impact of our interesting, innovative and exciting menus was there for everyone to see. There soon came a time when airlines stopped sending us their recommendations, preferring us to take the lead instead. The work became way more exciting and challenging for us this way, since we were not simply cooking the dishes suggested by them. There was a buzz in the kitchen and everyone was inspired to put in their best.

Some international airlines changed their menus twice a year, others only once a year. But domestic airlines such as Jet Airways and Air India changed their menu every day. We had to create six sets of menus for them that were rotated every day. And the entire set was refreshed every year.

With so much work to be done, I simply rolled up my sleeves and plunged headlong into the challenge. The entire team pitched in with new ideas and concepts as well. As always, I poured my heart and soul into it, and our business and ratings improved significantly as a result.

Soon, I was given the additional responsibility of Taj's other flight kitchens and was made the corporate chef for Taj SATS Flight Catering and Kitchens in Delhi, Chennai, Goa, Bangalore and Kolkata.

I was responsible for all the kitchens and each of the executive chefs reported to me. I had to be present for all the meal presentations in these kitchens and also had to be involved with other administrative aspects, in order to make them profitable.

Since I was on the Singapore Airlines culinary panel—that included chefs representing major cuisines such as Italian, Chinese, etc. in order to stay in the news with updates on menu and presentation—for nine years, from the third year onwards, I was invited to their annual global forum, where every chef would make a dish for a nine-course menu to be served to the participants at a grand dinner hosted by a five-star luxury hotel. The Singapore Airline sales and marketing team used to play a very active role at these forums. These two-day gala was organised to facilitate new ideas, and all the chefs would be asked about their plans for the year. Everyone gave their opinion, and Satish Arora, that laidback boy from Punjab, began to share his opinion on the elite global platform as well. I would talk about how zucchini could be an ingredient of the year, or how there was growing interest in Kerala cuisine and discuss how I wished to incorporate all of this in my menu for the year.

The setting for the final day of the global forum was spectacular. A team simulated service in the A380, with appetisers, amuse-bouche, soup, fish, main course, vegetarian dishes and dessert. As mentioned above, it was a nine-course menu and each chef was supposed to make one dish.

The panellists were seated on nine different tables. Each table had two empty chairs, one for the chef and the other for the air hostess. One by one, we would be called upon to present our dish and then go around each of the nine tables, explaining the what and why of the dish. I remember explaining to the members how Indian cuisine was essentially a game of spices, how Indian spices reacted to heat and water, how you could use ancient wisdom to cure a hangover and how my crab dish was created with the finest, most aromatic Indian spices with proven medicinal properties that would perk you up on a long-distance flight. I was nickamed Dr Arora!

The Crab Bhujne for Singapore Airlines was a baked masala crab with onion, garlic, chopped mushroom, crab meat, curry leaves, mustard seeds, turmeric powder, coriander powder, cumin powder, grated cheddar cheese, coconut milk and roasted coriander leaves. I made a stuffing and put this in the crab shell and then drizzled a little bit of coconut milk on top with shredded orange cheddar, after which the dish was baked.

For flights going out of Singapore to India or from India to Singapore, all my dishes were included. For flights going out of Singapore to USA, there was an American chef. Food was served with the name of the chef and his picture, whether it was Chinese, French, American, Japanese, Indo-European, Australian or Singaporean. This created a lot of buzz in the airline industry and later a few other airlines also started following this sort of a system.

I remember when the airplane model A380 was about to be launched, Singapore Airlines was the first to buy it. This was confidential information and we were given a guided tour of the interiors of the A380 to get an idea of the seats, the galleys, how the food was going to be heated, frozen, chilled. It was a big deal and I created one of my most dazzling menus for the launch of the A380, that year. On the Indian route, I made menus for first class using scallops, morel butter, grilled lobster and rack of lamb, which one normally did not get to see on airline menus. For vegetarians, I made a vegetarian Warki Badami Kofta, which had an almond-filled kofta with a silver leaf and saffron sauce. Dessert was ghewar with hazelnut kulfi. For business class, there was Paneer Mushroom Zabunesa, Dal Kabila, Broccoli Foogath and Three Pepper Pulao.

News of my successful stint with Singapore Airlines spread quickly, and other airlines, such as Air Malaysia, also started approaching us to create menus for them. I was associated with them for around two years. Three times a year, I would travel to Malaysia and create innovative Indian menus for their Sri Lanka, Pakistan, Bangladesh and India sectors. I also worked for South Africa Airlines, Air India and Jet Airways. I was invited to work for Air Mauritius as well, and I visited Mauritius thrice to train the chefs in preparing Indian food. The airlines started putting my photograph on their menu card, saying that these dishes had been created by Chef Satish Arora. My photograph and my name was flying around the world. I felt blessed and humbled.

To be honest, when I was asked to join the flight kitchen, I had felt a little unsure of my career prospects there, as I had always been a hotel chap. But I guess the goodwill that I had earned and my commitment to the Taj Group ensured that I was sought-after wherever they placed me. And what began as a temporary position became a permanent one and I was anointed Director, Food Productions, Taj Group.

Taj flight kitchen also catered to royal and Air Force One flights chartered for global dignitaries visiting Mumbai. That is how we got to make meals for former UK Prime Minister John Major, the Prince of Thailand, Margaret Thatcher and Bill Clinton, the Royal Navy of Oman and the kings of Brunei and Bhutan. We also handled outdoor catering for some global business conglomerates. All of this together amounted to 25,000–30,000 meals per day being cooked and served from that flight kitchen.

I finally stepped down from flight kitchen in 2016, after an eventful and creatively fulfilling chapter.

14

The Grand Raffles Experience

It has always been against my nature to wallow in negativity, or to allow negative thoughts to guide my actions. When I cook, I cook with my soul, and I serve that food with love. And I always believe that when you are true to your calling and to God, you will be blessed.

My years at the Taj flight kitchen were a blessing in ways I could never have imagined. All my initial misgivings melted away faster than butter on a hot griddle as more and more opportunities came my way, giving me confidence and fuelling my creative fire. My three-year stint with the prestigious Raffles Hotel, Singapore, was one such experience.

The Raffles is to Singapore what the Taj is to Mumbai. It's a symbol of regal, classical hospitality, elegance and an impeccable legacy. During my consultancy with Singapore Airlines, I would often drop by the Raffles Hotel, simply to say hello to the executive chef or a friendly manager, and to get an idea of how they defined hospitality.

In 2000, I visited the hotel with a chef from the Singapore Airlines kitchen, Jeremy Lim, and was introduced to the then executive and deputy chefs of the hotel, Jean Paul Naquin and Julien Bompard.

Bompard was familiar with my work as we had met during one of the grand Singapore Airlines dinner forums. We had a chat over tea and they invited me to eat at their Indian restaurant, Tiffin Room.

Tiffin Room was a reasonably popular restaurant at that time, mostly known for its buffet service, even though they had a few à-la-carte dishes as well. I took up the offer and tried out their buffet lunch and dinner on two consecutive days, and to be honest, I was quite disappointed. The flavours of the dishes were underwhelming and the menu wasn't very innovative. Some of the salads and mains on the lunch menu were repeated in the dinner buffet, and I did not expect to find something as basic as aloo mattar on a Raffles menu.

When they asked me for my opinion, I gave them my polite but honest feedback. I told them that given the kind of global and evolved clientele they serve at Raffles, the menu could be far more interesting and varied. Bompard wanted to know if I was interested in doing a food promotion for them as their brand ambassador.

It is not every day that one gets an opportunity like this, and I took it up without any hesitation.

It was decided that I would return in 2001 and do a ten-day food promotion for Raffles. I was to design a new menu for their Indian restaurant. This was right up my alley—by then I was familiar with the Singapore markets and knew where to source Indian herbs and spices and the freshest produce from. I began to work on a menu that would be worthy of Raffles' heritage and also appeal to their clientele.

I named the special promotion, 'A Culinary Journey of India'. My other food promotions that involved designing the menu and managing the presentation at Raffles, were named Spice Market and Indian Dhaba.

My priority was to introduce variety and avoid repetition. I created five menu sets for lunch and dinner for five days. Only one menu set would be repeated on the sixth day. I also planned for twenty different salads every day, ten for lunch and ten for dinner. I did the same for my choice of soups. For mains, I decided to do a joint of meat or fish to be carved during dinner, adding an element of showmanship. We also started serving kebabs for dinner, using the one tandoor that they had in the kitchen. We made half a dozen Indian sweets and some ice creams for dessert.

Creating a new menu was a great opportunity and a challenge. The introduction of kebabs was a hit with the guests. But with rising demand, we often struggled to keep pace with only one tandoor in the kitchen. Besides the four varieties of kebabs, the tandoor also had to be used to prepare rotis and naans. After struggling to keep up with the orders on the first day, I enlisted the help of their tandoor cook to prepare the batches of meat and prawns well in advance. We marinated them in different consistencies before service to reduce cooking time. The 120-cover restaurant was always full between 7 to 9 PM, and we needed to be prepared. I did not want to compromise on even one element—I was the hotel's brand ambassador after all, and so I tried out some of my tricks of the trade like using star anise and clove powder in the marinade and coating the meat heavily with the marinade to ensure everyone had juicy, flavoursome kebabs. It was hectic, challenging and extremely satisfying.

The buffet took off. Every time I visited the hotel, the press interviewed me about the thought process behind the menus I had created. I would always expound on the medicinal value of Indian herbs and spices and about my cooking philosophy—I didn't like using too much oil or too many spices, instead preferring to use techniques such as braising, steaming and stewing in order to enhance the flavour of food.

My association with Raffles extended to their cooking academy as well. They used to organise cookery demonstrations, where they invited a chef to teach twenty participants over the course of two days. I did three demonstrations at Raffles in 2001, 2002 and 2004. My focus for these demonstrations was to showcase the best of Indian cuisine, our ingredients and our techniques. I would dry roast and grind masalas, introducing the participants to the aroma of fresh spices, and would create innovative dishes such as Chicken Bhelpuri. I also taught students how to make a perfect chicken tandoori and chicken tikka for salads and appetizers. For vegetarians, I did a cashew nut and chickpea chaat with a freshly made tamarind sauce. I also showed them the correct way to make the popular butter chicken and paneer butter masala, to be served with a green peas pulao. I even showed them how to make the softest paneer at home. They loved it.

From green moong dal to beetroot halwa, chicken reshmi salad to paneer tikka, patrani machhi to chicken biryani, Bombay Pudding to paneer bhurji, dhansak to green peas kheer, I experimented with everything, and the participants were keen, curious and delighted.

Meanwhile, my new dishes on the Raffles menu also began to gain popularity. Particularly, the Lobster Palak Pakoda, Scallops Piri Piri, Prawns Saagwala, Lobster Kika, Patrani Machhi, Baked Oyster Indian-style, Murgh Hara Dhania, Potli Murgh, Amritsari Murgh Chole, Matka Murgh, Safed

Keema, Laila ki Pasliya (lamb chops) and the Lachilli Dhingri Aloo. I even put rajma palak and jackfruit biryani on the menu and created quite a stir in the foodie circle in Singapore. I was lucky to receive a lot of love and respect during the three years at Raffles, as did the Taj Group for making it possible for me to take on these assignments.

15

The Big (Star)Bucks

My years at Taj SATS were memorable for more than the various roles I played with international airlines. Rolling out the first-ever menu for the Indian debut of the world's most popular coffee chain was a highlight of my career at SATS, and a great honour. I still remember that day at my Taj SATS office, when I received a call from the CEO of the company. He told me that Starbucks was coming to India in partnership with the Tata Group and the first outlet would be launched at the heritage Elphinstone Building at Horniman Circle in the Fort area of Mumbai.

Howard Schultz, the chairman of Starbucks, was coming to India and we had just three months to prepare an Indian menu for the chain. I may have created menus for a five-star coffee shop and international airlines, but this was a completely different challenge! I was excited. I was familiar with Starbucks coffee and their food, and I knew it was a big deal to create a blockbuster menu for them. The Starbucks chef, Gary Martin, met me and told me outright that even though Starbucks served standardised items globally, he wanted my input on what could be done for the Indian market.

The cheesecakes, muffins and cookies were already part of the menu for India, but he was looking to add some customised savoury items to the menu—sandwiches, puff pastries with loads of local flavours and elements. I was impressed with how much Martin knew about Indian cuisine. He said he wanted to hold a workshop in Mumbai to develop a menu that married the best of Starbucks legacy with the best of Indian flavours. I put my thinking cap over my chef's hat.

I knew that we would have to work with corn breads and multigrain bread as per their international mandates, and not regular sliced white bread. But we could innovate with the filling. I was thinking along the lines of chilli-fried Chettinad masala, Malwani masala and some Goa-style Recheado masala. I also wanted to play around with a Parsi chicken cutlet and make it into a burger. I made elaborate notes and started a few trials on my own. We created a calzone with curry stuffing. A strudel with chana masala. We did a soya nuggets curry puff and were successful in creating a Parsi cutlet burger. We tasted all the items ourselves, collected feedback from the other chefs and the management, and came to the conclusion that with a little tweak here and there and a dash of my special masalas, these items could work very well for Starbucks.

On the day of the presentation, I explained each item carefully to Chef Martin, prepared the spice mixes in front of him and made him taste them so that he had a better idea of how they would eventually come together.

I could see that the gentleman was happy. He said, 'Usually when we make any Starbucks menu anywhere in the world, 30 per cent of the sales come from food and 70 per cent come from the beverages. In India, I think food will perform very well.'

I still remember the day, 19 October 2012, when Starbucks launched in India. Mr Ratan Tata, the chairman of the Tata Group, was supposed to inaugurate the outlet with

Mr Schultz, as the project was a joint venture of Starbucks and Tata Global Beverages. There was a grand party in an adjacent garden at Horniman Circle, which was attended by the who's who of Mumbai. We had made a temporary kitchen in the garden, as I wanted all items to be served hot.

We worked hard on creating a menu that would not only meet Starbucks' global standards of calorie counts, but also fit in with their costs. We also had to import some of the items and ingredients, such as butter croissants, pain au chocolat from France, blueberry muffin mix, apple vegan doughnut mix and crunchy feuilletine from Singapore.

The final menu, some of which is still going strong, looked somewhat like this: Basil tomato mozzarella sandwich made with brown bread, fresh basil, tomato and fresh mozzarella that melted on heating during service. People just loved it.

The other item which we tried, and the chef rated highly, was a chargrilled spiced potato-pepper ciabatta. We sliced potatoes and parboiled them. Then we marinated them with turmeric powder, chilli powder, lemon juice and salt, grilled them till they had visible grill marks, sliced the peppers and put it on a rye baguette, and then designed a very spicy tomato chutney to go with it. The chutney was made with tomato, mustard seeds, curry leaves, red chilli powder, lemon juice, sugar and salt. We put the chutney at the bottom of the baguette and then we placed the potatoes. On these potatoes, we had put orange cheddar cheese and when it was served at the counter, it was grilled, so that it would be nice and cheesy and stick to the potatoes.

We created a cheese and spinach sandwich and a corn brioche with corn mushroom salsa. For this, I made a corn and sliced mushroom salsa with a tomato-based sauce and herbs, and served it on the corn brioche.

We also made a tandoori paneer multigrain sandwich, which again was a hit. The tandoori chicken panini was also a hit. There was also a chatpata paratha wrap, which was a salty ajwain paratha to which I added grated cheese, masala and mixed vegetables. For non-vegetarians, we filled the paratha with shredded chicken. I suddenly thought of making a samosa, but with chocolate, and called it a 'Chocomosa'. This became quite popular at Starbucks. For this, we used khoya with elaichi, a bit of sugar and nuts and stuffed it in the puff. We fried it and dipped half of the samosa in melted chocolate and sprinkled white chocolate on the other half.

We also did a soya matar strudel. We took minced soya granules, made a fine Chettinad masala out of it and then made a strudel with it. There was also my favourite Parsi cutlet burger on the menu with mince lamb and chicken, but I added a twist to it—I dipped the patty in a masala egg slurry and fried it. I put this between the burger buns, which I had slathered with chilli mayonnaise spread. I also added a chicken ham slice and a cheddar cheese slice on top of the patty. Chef Gary loved it and named it 'Star club'.

We put a twist to the sausage roll as well. I took chicken mince and a lamb mince and just like we make seekh kabab, I first put the lamb mince on skewer, put it in a tandoor and when it was half-cooked, I took it out. I put the minced chicken on the lamb and then cooked in the tandoor. So we created a seekh kebab with two different meats. When you pull out the skewers from the kebabs, they make a hole. I filled it up with Philadelphia cream cheese, rolled the kebab into a puff pastry and made a sausage roll. It was an excellent product. We also made chicken and mushroom pie in the continental style, with a bit of white wine, onion, garlic and celery, herbs, a little cream, white sauce, and then stuffed the patty with cheese. It was very well-appreciated.

Regular cheese straws were given a makeover by using Konkani masala and were named Konkani Twists, with lamb for non-vegetarians and paneer for vegetarians. We also added some Thai elements to the menu by creating a tamarind peanut chicken calzone with Thai spices.

Gary was very happy with our efforts. He had pitched in with Starbucks classics such as lemon cheesecake, double chocolate muffin, loaf cake, lemon chocolate chip cup and apricot cake loaf. I added my two bits to the sweet menu with mawa elaichi croissant. I took the Parsi dessert known as khaja or gujia that is served during Holi, and used it as stuffing for the croissant. The innovations did not stop there. I used the fat red chillies used for making stuffed pickles in North India and made a chole turnover with it, which I then topped with mozzarella cheese. No one had seen Indian food and elements and techniques in this form at a cafe. And it worked.

It helped that Gary was extremely encouraging and wanted us to keep innovating and surprising our guests. I was making history at Starbucks every day with these food experiments. And it kept the adventurous chef in me alive and kicking!

Gary too put on a stellar show with his brownie, tart, chocolate soufflé gateaux, chocolate raspberry crunch cake, oatmeal raisin cookies, banana brownie, fuzzy chocolate chip cookies, apple cherry crumble, a coffee jelly tiramisu and an éclair with dry red chilli powder in the ganache.

On 19 October 2012, Starbucks opened its first café in India at a sprawling 4,500 sq. ft space in Elphinstone Building, Horniman Circle. The first day saw hundreds of people wait in queue for hours to get in. A week later, two more cafes were opened at the Taj Hotel and the Oberoi Mall. By the time I stepped down from Taj SATS in 2016, about forty cafes had already opened all around India. And Taj SATS was catering for all of them. Thanks to Starbucks, we were able to create a historic menu for a historic moment in the Indian hospitality industry.

Since its launch, the Starbucks menu has undergone several changes, with more seasonal items being added to the basic fare, and innovations to match our festive calendars. But the star-studded launch will always remain special simply because the stakes were so high.

Epilogue

In my life, whenever one door has closed, another has opened.

When you spend most of your life at one organisation, you are always worried about what your life will be like once you leave. What will you do when you wake up in the morning? Will you wear your chef whites? Will you make your to-do list for the day? Will you make yet another new dish with your favourite ingredients? All these thoughts crowded my mind, every now and then.

I had been appointed Director Food Production, Taj Hotels (south and west) in 1998, and then continued to be Director and Corporate Chef, In-flight Catering, when I was loaned to the flight kitchen officially. In that role, I had to take care of almost 38,000 meals a day—10,000 meals out of Delhi, 15,000 out of Mumbai, 5,000 out of Chennai, 3,000 out of Bengaluru, 4,000 out of Kolkata and 1,000 out of Goa. There were over 500 chefs who were reporting to me.

I was closely associated with the Taj, in one capacity or another, for almost fifty years. But I wanted to spend more time with my family, which had always been a struggle with all the travelling my work had entailed. The Taj had generously given me twelve extensions post my retirement in 2006, but I finally prepared to step down in 2015, after fifty years with the organisation.

After dedicating over five decades of my life to the hospitality industry, I still feel I have much more to explore and discover. I have worked tirelessly for the Indian hospitality industry, laying a solid foundation for it and popularising Indian cuisine the world over.

I also strongly believe that our catering colleges and institutes should receive international recognition. In an ever-evolving environment, we must invest time to secure the future of our industry with the active participation of all stakeholders.

I will end with a bold declaration: I have no regrets. My life has been a grand buffet, and as I stand here now, I look back at how each element has come together to create a delectable culinary and personal journey.

RECIPES

A Selection of My Favourite Recipes

Tali Arbi (Crisp Fried Colocassia)

My mother's recipe

Ingredients:

Arbi (Colocassia)	200 g
Red chilli paste	1½ tsp
Garlic paste	1 tbsp
Chaat masala	1 tsp
Lemon juice	1 tbsp
Salt	To taste
Semolina	To coat the arbi
Oil	120 ml

Method:

1. Boil the arbi with a little bit of salt in water till cooked. Remove and drain.
2. When cooled, peel and cut each piece in half.
3. Apply red chilli paste, garlic paste, salt and a little oil to the arbi. Keep aside for 15 minutes.
4. Press the marinated arbi between the palms to flatten.
5. Roll the arbi in semolina.
6. Fry in hot oil till crisp.
7. Serve sprinkled with chaat masala.

Cannelloni Arora

Ingredients:

Pasta Sheets	16
Stuffing	
Chopped onion	40 g
Chopped chives	30 g
Chopped garlic	20 g
Chopped celery	15 g
Thyme	a pinch
Chopped spinach (boiled)	600 g
Crushed black pepper	1 tbsp
Nutmeg powder	¼ tsp
Grated paneer	400 g
Pineapple (brunoise cut)	100 g
Red pepper (brunoise cut)	50 g
Fresh cream	200 ml
Butter	60 g
Salt	To taste
Olive oil	40 ml
Cheese Sauce	
Milk	700 ml
Flour	2 tbsp
Butter	80 g
Grated cheddar cheese	80 g
Cream cheese	60 g
Fresh cream	150 ml
Salt	To taste
Chopped parsley	3 g

Tomato Sauce

Chopped tomatoes	500 g
Tomato paste	1 tbsp
Tomato juice	400 ml
Chopped onion	30 g
Chopped garlic	15 g
Oregano	1 pinch
Sugar	1 tbsp
Salt	To taste
Olive oil	20 ml

To Finish

Grated cheddar cheese (to bake)	100 g
Chopped parsley (for garnish)	3 g

Method:

1. Heat water in a pan. Put a few drops of olive oil. When the water boils, add pasta sheets.
2. Simmer for almost 20 minutes, stirring at times. When done, refresh with cold water. Keep aside. Do not put sheets one on top of the other.
3. For the stuffing, heat oil and butter in a pan.
4. Add onion, garlic, celery and sauté till translucent. Add thyme.
5. Now put spinach and sauté on low flame for 15 minutes. Add paneer and sauté.
6. Put black pepper, nutmeg and red pepper. After four minutes, add salt and pineapple.
7. Add cream. Stir well.
8. Adjust seasonings and keep aside.
9. For the cheese sauce, heat milk in a pan.

10. In another pan, heat butter and then add flour. Sauté for 3 minutes. Add parsley followed by milk. Stir till it starts to thicken.
11. Add grated cheese and fresh cream. Adjust seasoning. Remove.
12. For the tomato sauce, heat oil and sauté onion and garlic in it.
13. Now add chopped tomatoes, oregano, and after 5 minutes, add tomato puree. Then add the tomato juice.
14. Put sugar, salt and after 5 minutes, remove.
15. To present, grease a serving dish with butter.
16. Arrange cannelloni rolls with stuffing. Cover with cheese sauce, then pour tomato sauce on top of it.
17. Sprinkle with grated cheese on top. Gratinate till the top is brown and bubbling. Serve sprinkled with chopped parsley.

Gosht Keema Ghotala

Ingredients:

Diced lamb	500 g
Garlic paste	25 g
Turmeric powder	1 tsp
Cardamom (green)	6
Cloves	6
Black cardamom	10
Chopped onion	70 g
Garlic paste	20 g
Ginger paste	20 g
Red chilli paste	30 g
Cumin seeds	1 tsp
Chopped green chillies	2
Red chilli powder	2 tsp
Coriander powder	2 tbsp
Cumin powder	1 tbsp
Chopped tomatoes	200 g
Tomato puree	1 tbsp
Turmeric powder	1 tsp
Garam masala powder	1 tsp
Lemon juice	1 tbsp
Lamb liver	150 g
Eggs	8
Salt	To taste
Roasted saunf (fennel) powder	1 tbsp
Desi ghee	100 ml
Chopped coriander leaves	3 g

Method:

1. Apply garlic paste and turmeric to lamb.
2. Put lamb in a pan. Cover with water.

3. Add cardamom, clove and black cardamom. Simmer till the lamb is cooked.
4. Remove lamb pieces. Strain stock and keep to make gravy.
5. Melt ghee in a pan and crackle cumin seeds in it. Add onion and sauté till brown.
6. Add ginger-garlic paste and sauté for 5 minutes. Add red chilli paste and sauté for another 5 minutes. Add turmeric powder.
7. Now add tomatoes and cook till tomatoes are soft. Add tomato puree. Sauté for 5 minutes.
8. Add lamb and mix well. Add reserved lamb stock as required to make gravy. Add salt to taste.
9. When gravy is simmering, add coriander powder, cumin powder and liver. Let it simmer for 10 minutes, till the gravy becomes thicker.
10. Add lemon juice, saunf powder, chopped coriander leaves.
11. Beat eggs with red chilli powder, salt and coriander leaves. Make a scramble.
12. Mix the lamb with the scrambled egg and serve.

Idli Chaat Chatori

Ingredients:

Semolina	200 g
Yogurt	75 g
Salt	To taste
Mustard seeds	½ tsp
Roasted crushed curry leaves	4
Eno (fruit salt)	½ tsp
Oil	To fry idli

Tamarind Chutney

Tamarind	70 g
Dates	70 g
Jaggery	70 g
Roasted cumin powder	1 tsp
Red chilli powder	1 tsp
Black salt	½ tsp

Assembly of Chaat

Beaten yogurt	200 ml
Roasted cumin powder	1 tsp
Red chilli powder	1 tsp
Tamarind chutney	2 tbsp
Chopped parsley	1 tsp
Chopped prunes	20 g

Method:

1. Mix semolina, beaten yogurt, salt, mustard seeds and curry leaves.
2. Add a little water to make a semi-pourable batter. Keep aside for 30 minutes.

3. Take idli steamer (mini moulds) and put butter on them and put them over heat.
4. Grease idli moulds with a little oil.
5. Now mix batter with Eno. Mix well.
6. Pour batter in moulds and steam. It will take 15–20 minutes to steam.
7. Remove idlis from moulds.
8. Heat oil and shallow fry idli till crispy.
9. Put idlis in a bowl. Put yogurt, prunes, powdered masalas, parsley and mix well.
10. Before serving, sprinkle tamarind chutney.

Tamarind Chutney

1. Put dates, jaggery, tamarind in a pan and cover with water. Bring to a boil, then simmer till cooked and tender. Strain.
2. Add all the other ingredients and salt. Mix well.

JRD Club

Ingredients:

Multigrain bread slices	4

Filling:

Shredded roast chicken	120 g
Shredded English ham	80 g
Emmenthal cheese	60 g
Rocket leaves	6 g
Fried egg (well-done over easy)	2
Crispy fried bacon bits	20 g
Salt	To taste
Butter	To spread
Cocktail sauce	3 tbsp
Tomato slices	50 g

Method:

1. Toast bread, apply butter.
2. Mix the chicken, ham and bacon with cocktail sauce.
3. Put rocket leaves on two slices of bread.
4. Then put the chicken mixture on top, followed by fried egg and tomato slices.
5. Cover with the remaining two slices of bread.
6. Grill till golden. Serve.

Lasagna Royale

Made especially for Prince Charles' party in Warwick Castle, England, for Asian industrialists

Ingredients:

Big, long aubergines	4
Chopped onion	100 g
Chopped garlic	20 g
Chopped celery	20 g
Thyme	¼ tsp
Boiled black-eyed beans	75 g
Diced paneer	100 g
Sliced mushroom	120 g
Boiled broccoli florets	100 g
Red pepper (brunoised)	30 g
Crushed walnuts	30 g
Crushed black pepper	1 tsp
Fresh cream	120 ml
Butter	40 g
Coconut milk powder	2 tbsp
Fine dices of aubergine	100 g
Chopped parsley	3 g
Cream cheese	50 g
Salt	To taste

Coconut Sauce

Flour	35 g
Butter	35 g
Thin coconut milk	700 ml
Fresh cream	100 ml
White pepper powder	1 tsp
Salt	To taste

Tomato Sauce

Chopped red tomatoes	500 g
Chopped onion	70 g
Chopped garlic	20 g
Oregano	1 tsp
Tomato juice	250 ml
Sugar	1 tbsp
Salt	To taste

To Finish

Grated cheddar cheese	200 g
Chopped parsley	3 g

Method:

1. Clean and wash aubergines. Cut into long slices (not very thin). Add salt. Keep aside for 30 minutes.
2. Grill aubergine. Do not fully cook them. Keep aside.

Filling

1. Heat butter. Sauté onion, garlic, celery till translucent. Add thyme.
2. Put mushroom and sauté for 4 minutes. Add diced aubergine. Cook for 4 minutes.
3. Add broccoli, paneer, beans, pepper, walnut and sauté for 5–6 minutes.
4. Put coconut milk powder. Mix well.
5. Now add black pepper, salt, fresh cream, cream cheese and parsley. Sauté for 5 minutes. Keep aside.

Coconut Sauce:

1. Melt butter, add flour. Sauté till flavours come out.
2. Add coconut milk (consistency like regular milk). Stir well.

3. Add pepper, salt and cream. Keep aside.

Tomato Sauce:

1. Melt butter. Sauté onion and garlic for 6 minutes. Add oregano.
2. Now add the tomatoes. Sauté till cooked. Add juice, seasonings and sugar.

Assembly:

1. Take a platter. Grease it with butter.
2. Arrange slices of aubergine.
3. Put filling on slices. Moisten with coconut sauce.
4. Cover with slices of aubergine.
5. Now put filling on these slices and cover with more slices of aubergine.
6. Cover slices with coconut sauce. Sprinkle a little tomato sauce on the coconut sauce.
7. Put grated cheese on top and gratinate it.
8. Serve sprinkled with chopped parsley.

Lobster Kika

Ingredients:

Lobster	3
Chopped onion	60 g
Chopped spring onion	30 g
Chopped garlic	35 g
Chopped ginger	20 g
Chopped green chillies	2
Cumin seeds	1 tsp
Mustard seeds	1 tsp
Curry leaves	6
Red chilli powder	2 tsp
Chopped coriander leaves	4 g
Cream cheese	50 g
Fresh cream	160 ml
Coriander powder	1 tsp
Crushed black pepper	1 tsp
Chopped mushrooms	200 g
Boiled spinach puree	50 g
Chopped walnuts	25 g
Cumin powder	½ tsp
Nutmeg powder	A pinch
Butter	120 g
Grated cheddar cheese	100 g
Salt	To taste
Oil	40 ml
Vinegar	2 tbsp
Tomato paste	1 tsp
Almond milk	100 ml

Method:

1. Bring a large pot of water to boil with vinegar in it. Add the lobster and boil for 30 minutes. The shell will turn to a bright red colour.
2. Remove the lobster from the pot. Cut each lobster in half, length-wise. Remove the lobster meat from the shell and keep aside.
3. Cut the lobster meat in dices.
4. Heat pan and add oil. Crackle cumin, mustard seeds and curry leaves.
5. Add 30 g onion and sauté for 4 minutes. Add 20 g garlic, ginger, 1 chopped green chilli and sauté till translucent. Add 1 tsp red chilli powder, ½ tsp coriander powder, salt and half of the coriander leaves.
6. Now add cream cheese, 60 ml fresh cream and diced lobster. Adjust seasoning.
7. Sauté well this onion cream mixture. Keep aside.
8. In a pan, sauté spring onion and the remaining garlic in 60 g butter.
9. When browned, add mushrooms and sauté well till the water released from the mushrooms dries up.
10. Then add spinach and sauté on low flame. Add black pepper, walnuts, 40 ml cream, salt and nutmeg powder. Add cumin powder and ½ tsp coriander powder and cook over simmering heat.
11. Sauté 30 g onion in 60 g butter till translucent.
12. Add tomato paste and after 1 minute, add cream. Add almond milk and salt. Simmer till the sauce is of pouring consistency.
13. Take the lobster shells and put the mushroom mixture at the base of it.
14. Now put the lobster mixture on top of the mushrooms and fill up the shells.

15. Pour the sauce over it.
16. Sprinkle cheddar cheese all over.
17. Bake in a broiler or salamander oven till the top becomes a nice golden colour.

Lobster Palak Pakoda

Ingredients:

Lobster meat (diced)	300 g
Chopped spinach	50 g
Cumin seeds	1 tsp
Garlic paste	20 g
Red chilli powder	1 tsp
Chopped green chilli	1
Turmeric powder	½ tsp
Lemon juice	1 tsp
Besan flour	150 g
Salt	To taste
Oil	To deep-fry
Water	To make batter
Chaat masala	½ tsp

Chutney

Pomegranate juice	1 tbsp
Mayonnaise	2 tbsp
Tamarind pulp	1 tsp
Black salt powder	½ tsp
Melted jaggery	1 tbsp
Chopped parsley	1 tsp
Red chilli powder	1 tsp
Roasted cumin powder	1 tsp
Salt	To taste

Method:

1. Wash, clean and pat dry lobster dices. Keep the shells.
2. Clean, wash spinach. Chop.

3. Take a bowl. Put cumin, garlic, red chilli, turmeric, green chilli, lemon juice, besan, salt, chaat masala and make a pouring batter with water.
4. Now put lobster and spinach in it. Mix well.
5. Heat oil. Using a teaspoon, put the lobster spinach mixture into the hot oil like fritters. Remove when the fritters turn lightly golden. Remove.
6. Deep-fry again till golden. Serve with chutney.
7. For the chutney, mix all the ingredients in a bowl. The mixture should be of pouring consistency.

Makhmali Murgh Goli

Ingredients:

For the chicken balls

Minced chicken	300 g
Boiled potato	75 g
Cumin seeds	1 tsp
Red chilli powder	1 tsp
Chopped green chilli	1
Roasted cumin powder	1 tsp
Chaat masala	1 tsp
Chopped coriander leaves	3 g
Chopped walnuts	30 g
Salt	To taste
Oil	60 ml

For the assembly

Butter	50 g
Brunoise of red pepper	30 g
Brunoise of stuffed green olive	25 g
Philadelphia cream cheese	2 tbsp
Mayonnaise	1 tbsp
Chopped green chilli	1
Black salt	½ tsp
Chaat masala	½ tsp
Red chilli powder	½ tsp
Fresh cream	1½ tbsp
Chopped coriander leaves	2 g
Chopped garlic	15 g
Chopped ginger	15 g
Mustard seeds	½ tsp
Salt	To taste

Method:

1. In a bowl, put minced chicken, boiled potato, cumin seeds, red chilli, green chilli, cumin powder, chaat masala, walnuts, coriander leaves and mix well. Add salt to taste.
2. Make small balls, or golis, out of this mixture. Steam them for 10 minutes. Remove.
3. Heat oil, sauté the balls till they are golden.
4. Take a pan, add butter. Sauté garlic, ginger till golden.
5. Add mustard seeds, curry leaves, and after 5 minutes, add red pepper, green olive, coriander leaves, green chillies and powdered masalas. Sauté well. Add the chicken koftas.
6. Place the sautéed koftas in a bowl and add Philadelphia cream cheese, cream, mayonnaise. Mix well. Adjust seasonings as per taste.
7. Sprinkle coriander leaves and serve hot or cold as desired.

Murgh Bhelpuri

Ingredients:

Chicken Tikka

Diced chicken	250 g
Yogurt	150 g
Garlic paste	25 g
Ginger paste	20 g
Lemon juice	½ of a lemon
Roasted besan powder	1½ tbsp
Red chilli paste	1 tsp
Salt	To taste
Oil	1 tbsp

Chutney

Dates	200 g
Jaggery	100 g
Tamarind	100 g
Roasted cumin powder	1 tsp
Red chilli powder	1 tsp
Black salt	½ tsp
Water	To cover

Main Ingredients

Chopped onion	50 g
Chopped green chillies	30 g
Diced boiled potato	100 g
Chopped coriander leaves	3 g
Crushed peanuts	20 g
Puffed rice flakes	120 g
Nylon sev	40 g

Salt	To taste
Coriander powder	½ tsp
Red chilli powder	½ tsp

Method:

1. Marinate chicken with garlic, ginger, lemon juice, red chilli paste, besan, salt and yogurt.
2. Mix and keep for 30 minutes.
3. For the chutney, take a pan with dates, tamarind and jaggery. Add water and simmer till all the ingredients are soft.
4. Strain and add the powdered spices and black salt. Mix well and set aside.
5. Skewer marinated chicken and cook in tandoor for 15–20 minutes.
6. Remove chicken from skewers, cut in small dices. Keep aside.
7. In a mixing bowl, put all the items listed in main ingredients section.
8. Add diced chicken, mix well.
9. Now add 2 tbsp of the date chutney. Mix well. You can adjust the chutney according to your preference.
10. Serve garnished with chopped coriander leaves.

Mutton Masala Burger

Ingredients:

Roast lamb (thin slices)	400 g

Masala

Chopped onion	30 g
Garlic paste	15 g
Chopped ginger	15 g
Chopped green chillies	2
Red chilli paste	1½ tbsp
Chopped tomatoes	80 g
Tomato puree	30 g
Turmeric powder	1 tsp
Coriander powder	1 tsp
Cumin powder	1 tsp
Star anise powder	¼ tsp
Kitchen King masala	1 tsp
Chaat masala	1 tsp
Crushed black peppercorn	1 tsp
Chopped coriander leaves	2 g
Salt	To taste
Oil	40 ml
Juice of ¼ lemon	

Finishing

Burger buns	4
Butter	To apply
Potato chips	To serve

Method:

Filling

1. Add oil to a pan. Sauté onion, ginger, green chillies till golden.
2. Add garlic paste and sauté. Add red chilli paste and then chopped tomatoes. Sauté well till the tomatoes are well-cooked.
3. Now add the tomato puree and, after 2 minutes, add powdered masalas and turmeric. Sauté well.
4. Put lamb slices and sauté on low flame till the lamb is smeared with the masala.
5. Add coriander leaves and lemon juice.

Assembly

1. Cut buns in half.
2. Apply butter on all sides and toast them in a pan till they are a little brown.
3. Add filling on the base of a bun and cover with the top half.
4. Serve with potato chips.

Safed Murgh Biryani

Served to former US President Bill Clinton

Ingredients:

Diced chicken	500 g
Garlic paste	30 g
Ginger paste	20 g
Green chilli paste	20 g
Cashew paste	100 g
Yogurt	120 g
Cream cheese	60 g
Green cardamom powder	1 tbsp
Mace powder	1 tsp
White pepper powder	1 tsp
Fresh cream	100 ml
Salt	To taste
Oil	2 tbsp

Biryani

Sliced onion	120 g
Chopped garlic	20 g
Chopped ginger	20 g
Green chillies	5 g
Cumin seeds	1 tsp
Chopped mint	5 g
Chopped coriander leaves	5 g
Whole black pepper	1 tbsp
Coconut milk powder	2 tbsp
Water	400 ml
Fresh cream	80 ml
Salt	To taste

Ghee	100 g
Basmati rice	250 g
Cardamom powder	1 tsp
Garam masala powder	1 tsp
Kewra water	3 drops

Method:

1. Marinate chicken with yogurt, garlic, green chilli paste, cashew paste, cream, green cardamom powder, mace powder, salt, oil and cream cheese. Keep aside for 30 minutes.
2. Wash, clean and soak rice in water.
3. Put ghee in a pan. Sauté chicken till juices are sealed. Keep aside.
4. Now take a pan, melt ghee in it. Put onion, garlic, ginger, green chillies and sauté till translucent.
5. Add cumin seeds, then chicken. Sauté well.
6. Add cardamom powder, garam masala, mint, coriander leaves and sauté.
7. Mix coconut powder in water.
8. Drain the soaked rice and add to the chicken. Sauté for 3 minutes. Add coconut powder and water mixture and mix well. Simmer till rice starts to cook. Add kewra water.
9. When half done, add cream.
10. Cook till rice and chicken are done. Serve hot.

ACKNOWLEDGEMENTS

Chandrima Pal, co-author and a dynamic professional with a powerful pen. Gitanjali Gurbaxani, for her initiative and enthusiasm in getting this book done. Ajit Kerkar, ex-chairman, MD, Indian Hotels Company, and my mentor; it was his faith in me that made me the youngest executive chef in the world when I was only twenty-six years old. Mernosh Kapadia of Tata Sons, who mentored me to achieve the best. Chef Miguel Arcanjo Mascarenhas, senior executive chef, from who I took over as executive chef. Camellia Panjabi, the brains behind the specialty restaurants at the Taj Group, from whom I learned the nitty-gritty of the business. I would also like to thank Vir Sanghvi, celebrity food writer, for always recognising my work.

Thanks to my parents, whose blessings helped me arrive at my destination. Puneet Arora, my son, my support system, who always wished for me and encouraged me to do a book on my culinary journey. Every step he takes in his career brings me joy. His wife, Dr Gayatri Arora, a food connoisseur who inspired me to dream big. My darling daughter, Kanika Gangwani, the most genuine food critic I could ask for, who always enjoyed my innovations. Her husband, Dr Vinod Gangwani, a true gourmand. My grandchildren Natania Arora and Neev Gangwani, who love every little thing I cook for them and keep inspiring me.

Last but not the least, my kitchen brigade at the Taj and the chef fraternity of India.

INDEX

ABOUT THE AUTHOR

Satish Arora put Indian cuisine on the global fine-dining map when the world was yet to discover life beyond tikka masala. During his five-decade-long stint at the Taj kitchens in Mumbai, Arora brought his distinctive culinary innovations to the country's most high-profile banquets catering to world leaders, royalty, and men and women of eminence from across continents.